TIPS AND OTHER BRIGHT IDEAS FOR ELEMENTARY SCHOOL LIBRARIES

TIPS
AND OTHER
BRIGHT
IDEAS

or Elementary
chool
ibraries

Volume 4

te Vande Brake, Editor

 LINWORTH

AN IMPRINT OF ABC-CLIO, LLC
Santa Barbara, California • Denver, Colorado • Oxford, England

Copyright 2010 by ABC-CLIO, LLC

Library of Congress Cataloging-in-Publication Data

Tips and other bright ideas for elementary school libraries.
  Volume 4 / Kate Vande Brake, editor.
     p. cm.
  ISBN 978-1-58683-416-6 (acid-free paper) — ISBN 978-1-58683-417-3
(ebook)   1. Elementary school libraries—United States—Administration.
I. Vande Brake, Kate.
  Z675.S3T493   2010
  025.1'978222—dc22   2010011049

ISBN: 978-1-58683-416-6
EISBN: 978-1-58683-417-3

14   13   12   11   10   1   2   3   4   5

This book is also available on the World Wide Web as an eBook.
Visit www.abc-clio.com for details.

Linworth
An Imprint of ABC-CLIO, LLC

ABC-CLIO, LLC
130 Cremona Drive, P.O. Box 1911
Santa Barbara, California 93116-1911

This book is printed on acid-free paper ∞

Manufactured in the United States of America

TABLE
OF CONTENTS

INTRODUCTION

One decade into the 21st century, school libraries across the United States are leaders in technology innovation. Today's libraries are riding the tail of the Internet and the World Wide Web to blaze an amazing path of technology and information assets for our young patrons. From Wikis to Nings to library Web pages chock-full of resources and interactive tools, libraries have come a very long way in a very short time.

Librarians are leaders in the field of information literacy and information technology. They teach their patrons to embrace new technologies. Today's librarians are media specialists—experts in books and media, in inquiry and research, and in information technology. Although most adults can learn new technologies on an as-needed basis, library media specialists stay about 10 steps ahead, ready for each new query—and armed with possible leads to find answers.

Library media specialists' jobs are complicated by today's economic situation. Our attitudes about how we spend our time and our budgets are highly influenced by the continuing budget decreases and rumors that circulate regarding which positions will be cut each spring as our districts contemplate programs to sacrifice.

In the early 1990s, the first volume of *Shoptalk: Ideas for Elementary School Librarians* was published to provide an easy and helpful reference book for librarians. Subsequent editions offered more great money- and time-saving tips for school librarians. A new edition is now born as library media specialists have continued to offer their advice, practical knowledge, and experience to a vast network of lifelong learners eager to improve their media programs and continue to positively impact their school communities.

Although technology has changed significantly, elementary school librarians are still responsible for the management of their media centers and the volunteers and staff who help with the daily operations. It is up to us to advocate for our media centers through programs, special events, and creative activities.

The elementary librarian is more immersed in teaching the inquiry process and information literacy skills than ever before. Literacy skills are more crucial than ever as students continue to learn in this complex, media-rich world. It continues to be a goal to build and maintain an inclusive and attractive atmosphere and climate in the media center as we meet the needs of a very diverse population of students. Making the space conducive to learning, collaborating, networking, and enticing and engaging readers requires creative thinking on our part. Organizing and reorganizing magazines and books, arranging furniture to facilitate learning, setting up for the next class, designing displays promoting new books, and designing bulletins boards is challenging work. Maintaining supplies and equipment for teachers and students who know the library is "the place to be" sets another challenge for the school librarian. Librarians are often responsible for our own budgets and must balance the need for new books with the need to replace old books. Some of us are fortunate enough to have books processed for us, but many times we must find the time to process our own acquisitions. Often we must dust the books, fix book bindings, tape ripped pages, and dry the occasional wet page.

Collaboration with other teachers is encouraged and is more and more commonplace in many schools today. Technology, already identified as a necessary skill for today's library media specialist (LMS), is a key component of successful collaboration, whether it is the main mode of communication between the librarian and the collaborating teacher or the underlying element of the collaborative project. Technology is used to stretch students' imaginations, to promote the culminating event of a collaborative project, or to invite participation from other students and parents.

The librarian of today finds herself at the center of her school. She is always discovering new materials for other teachers in the building; she is the bridge between grade levels and can challenge the younger students while encouraging older students. She is given the opportunity to see the big picture and can relay important information back to her administration and peers.

The tips included in this edition of *Tips and Other Bright Ideas for Elementary School Libraries* showcase the ingenuity and creativity of today's librarian. Recognizing that the "definition" of elementary school varies from district to district, the editor has included relevant tips from middle school librarians in this edition.

The tips in this book are organized into the following nine sections:

- Managing the Library
- Working with Students in the Library
- Teaching Research Skills
- Collaborating with Teachers
- Using Technology in the Library
- Promoting Reading
- Building Positive Public Relations
- Working with Helpers

Please use the creative and practical tips included in this volume to help provide you with fresh ideas that will solve some of your ongoing challenges or simply make your job easier.

Some of these tips may sound familiar because you are already implementing similar ideas in your own media center. You probably have other great ideas though, so please submit your ideas to Library Media Connection. You can contact LMC online at http://www.linworth.com/lmc. Thanks for sharing your expertise through collaborating to strengthen library media programs across this country for students, teachers, and colleagues.

MANAGING
THE
LIBRARY

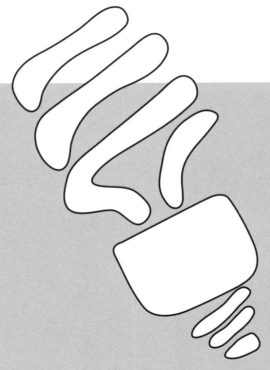

I s your library 21st-century-learner-friendly? Read on for some ideas and suggestions to make the most of your space and maximize your management skills. Employing some of these tips may help make the systems and organization of your library smooth sailing.

The tips included in this section have been divided into the following topics:

- Administration
- Arrangement
- Appearance and Order
- Displays and Bulletin Boards
- Supplies
- Equipment
- Acquisitions
- Processing Books and Materials

ADMINISTRATION

Business Cards

Business cards are our professional interface with the world. Every librarian needs business cards, even if they are homemade. Office supply stores carry blank decorative business cards that can be run through a home printer. A Google Images search will yield plenty of library-themed art to be printed on simple card stock.

 Sheryl Kindle Fullner, Nooksack Valley Middle School, Everson, Washington • April/May 2007

Media Bee

Instead of a Quilting Bee, schedule a Media Bee as part of monthly district library meetings. The Bee rotates through all the libraries. Each building librarian in turn selects a job that could be tackled in a 30- to 45-minute time slot and prepares an appropriate number of staplers, scissors, computers, and so on, so that peer librarians can make a big dent in those jobs that are too daunting to tackle alone—for example, the nefarious *back room*.

 Sheryl Kindle Fullner, Nooksack Valley Middle School, Everson, Washington • October 2008

Post-a-Note

There are several inexpensive Web-based companies from which to buy postcards. Design your own media center postcards and use them to send friendly notes to staff, parents, and others. Put your favorite reading quote along with your name, the name of your school, and your e-mail address or phone number. Keep them by your computer, and you will use them often!

Catherine Trinkle, Hickory Elementary, Avon, Indiana • August/September 2008

Thank-You Supplies

Stock your desk drawer with a box of thank-you cards, a box of sympathy cards, a box of blank note cards with a multipurpose design (e.g., flowers, mountain scenes, etc.), and a book of "forever" stamps. You will then have these materials handy for sending thank-you notes to colleagues, administrators, sales reps, and others who go out of their way to support your library program. It will also facilitate sending sympathy cards and other greetings to coworkers.

Amy Pickett, Ridley High School, Folsom, Pennsylvania • August/September 2008

Be Prepared

At the beginning of the school year, type out a checklist for library substitutes and laminate it, with one copy for the office and one copy for your library. In addition to the various user names and passwords, describe where light switches, thermostats, computer switches, and copier switches are located. Spell out storm procedures such as unplugging cords or how to use surge protectors (and where they are located). Describe where the emergency procedure folder is located in the event of fires, terrorist attacks, floods, blizzards, earthquakes, and so on. Include a few jobs that always need to be done.

Sheryl Kindle Fullner, Nooksack Valley Middle School, Everson, Washington • January/February 2009

Logging In

To simplify instructions for a substitute, do a screen capture (usually Shift+Print Screen) of each step of the log-on process. Then paste and print these visuals in sequence in your sub folder. There is nothing like coming back from a bad illness or accident to find that a sub has not been able to log on, and the library is littered with sticky notes of students' first names and vague book titles. In our district, log-on IDs change regularly, so the folder needs to be updated every time the password changes.

Sheryl Kindle Fullner, Nooksack Valley Middle School, Everson, Washington • May/June 2009

Measuring Up

Library workers often need to measure things. Instead of reaching for a ruler or tape measure, attach a measuring gauge to the outside top edge your keyboard drawer for instant availability. Rulers and tapes that are as thin as a piece of cardboard are easy to find, or just photocopy any flat tape measure onto an overhead transparency and trim to fit your space. Hold securely with wide library tape wrapping around the edge of the drawer.

Sheryl Kindle Fullner, Nooksack Valley Middle School, Everson, Washington • May/June 2009

Drill and Practice

Keep informational tidbits you want to remember on a daily calendar such as Microsoft Outlook. Enter the item so that it repeats itself for a few weeks or even months. Each morning, the hint or new term is visible, so that you can learn new terms or ideas quickly. It's great for copyright ideas from Carol Simpson, for information from Joe Huber of LMC, for terms such as OSS (open source software), or even for new Web sites.

Donna Walters, Valparaiso (Indiana) High School
• May/June 2009

Tracking the Notes

Taking a few minutes to note personal successes, dissatisfactions, and potential ideas for the future—as well as soliciting comments and suggestions from others at the conclusion of library media program events—is most helpful. Place the notes along with the CD-ROM that stores documents related to the event (flyers, emails, letters, etc.) in a binder for easy retrieval.

Vanessa Fortenberry, Stoneview Elementary,
Lithonia, Georgia • November/December 2008

Meeting an Author at a Convention?

If you are attending a convention and hope to meet an author, make sure you take a camera. Ahead of time, purchase a mat for a 4 by 6-inch photo. Have the author sign the mat and take a photo. After the convention, you can use the mat to frame the photo and create a display in the library.

Mary Croix Ludwick, Thomas Haley Elementary K-5,
Irving ISD, Texas • November/December 2007

Germ Fighting

If library aides or volunteer helpers use your computer, keep some germ-killing hand wipes available during flu and cold season. Your school nurse will probably have individual packets of these. Use one to go over the keyboard, the mouse, and even the gel pads to cut down on contagion. Use one on the phone as well.

 Sheryl Kindle Fullner, Nooksack Valley Middle School, Everson, Washington • October 2007

ⒶⓇⓇⒶⓃⒼⒺⓂⒺⓃⓉ

Favorite Character Paint Sticks

Here's a fun way to help primary students find their favorite series books more quickly and easily. Get some paint-stirring sticks from your local lumberyard or decorating store. Spray-paint them bright colors and attach a laminated picture of the series book character to one end. Put the sticks on the shelves in the middle of the series books. The sticks will make locating and shelving books easier, plus they brighten up your picture book collection!

Joan Arth, Alexander Doniphan Elementary,
Liberty, Missouri • March 2006

By the Colors

Colored transparent spine labels are a great way to distinguish special categories in your library. I use green to cover the spine labels of the reference collection and red for the professional books for the staff. This is especially helpful if you have student aides assisting you in circulation and reshelving duties. The colored transparent spine labels are available from most library supply vendors.

Marilyn Eanes, Hopewell Middle School,
Round Rock, Texas • March 2007

Holiday Book Collection

After years of searching through the shelves for all of the holiday books as each holiday rolled around, I decided to use a separate section of shelving for all the holiday books, grouped by the appropriate holiday. The shelves are arranged by month, and each group of books has its own holiday sticker on the spine.

My primary-grades children no longer have to ask, "Where is a Halloween book?" and my aide and I don't have to scour the shelves six or seven times a year. Circulation of these books has increased tremendously, and the children check them out all year long because they can easily find the books.

Kim Belknap, Penn London Elementary,
West Grove, Pennsylvania • November/December 2007

Using Pictures to Find Nonfiction Books

We noticed that our first grade students had difficulty finding books when they were first introduced to the nonfiction area. They would continually ask for the same types of books each week. To help them with this process, we placed clip art pictures near the shelves with popular nonfiction topics so that they could easily spot the books. For instance, a small dog picture was placed next to the shelf with all of the books about dogs. The students are more self-sufficient in finding books in this area, and they can easily remember their favorite sections from checkout to checkout.

Paige Edwards, Barksdale Elementary,
Plano, Texas • October 2006

Series Series

Our students are very interested in reading books, especially novels, that are part of a series. Although we have the series information in the library catalog, it is difficult for the "browsers" to locate this information on the shelves. To help those students, we put labels with the name of the series and the volume, if available, across the top of the spines of the books. That way, as students are browsing, they can easily see what books are in a series and in which order they should be read.

Karen Burch, William Chrisman High School,
Independence, Missouri • October 2007

APPEARANCE AND ORDER

Rolling through Weeding

Tired of sore knees or sitting on the floor while working in the stacks to weed, read the shelves, or complete inventory? Use a garden/weeding cart with a seat that lifts up. This will allow you to store a laptop computer inside and run the scanner cord up through the handle area. You can be completely wireless and mobile during inventory time!

Terri Lent, Patrick Henry High School, Ashland, Virginia • April/May 2008

Color Coordination

Many school libraries have neutral, monochromatic, or dated color schemes. One bright color can pump a huge amount of energy into the space. Our school color is purple, so at garage sales, I keep an eye out for vases, plastic containers, garlands, lights, banners, buckets—even purple spray paint—that might be put to library use. With many matching colored items in our cupboards, our library always looks coherent, trendy, and vibrant with very little expense.

Sheryl Kindle Fullner, Nooksack Valley Middle School, Everson, Washington • April/May 2007

Slip Sliding Away

Use furniture slides to move bookshelves without having to take the books off of them first. Slides are available at the hardware store in a variety of sizes and allow you to move heavy furniture easily and without having to rely on your maintenance crew to help you out!

Catherine Trinkle, Hickory Elementary, Avon, Indiana • April/May 2008

Take Your Jacket Off and Stay Awhile

When weeding the collection, make special books circulate longer by removing tattered dust jackets. Often the clean, bright hardcover underneath can allow the loved book to stand up to several more checkouts!

Tammy Sauls, Orangewood Christian School, Maitland, Florida • August/September 2007

Trash to Treasure

Don't throw away those zippered plastic bags in which linens come packaged. They make great containers for bulletin board items, puppets, seasonal decorations, and the like. They take up very little space and can even be stored in a file cabinet, alphabetized by subject with your other lesson materials. Not only does the plastic protect your possessions; you can also easily see what each bag contains.

Betsy Long, Doby's Mill Elementary, Camden, South Carolina • February 2008

Organizing Company Catalogs

To organize vendor catalogs, use a permanent Sharpie pen (this writes on all types of covers) to label the catalog. On the top left of the front cover, I write the name of the company. On the top middle, I write the type of catalog. On the top right, I put the date the catalog was received. File these in Princeton magazine files labeled with the following categories: A-V Equipment, Book Sale, Foreign Language, Computer, Library Publisher, Library Supplies, Multimedia (all types of formats), Prebound and Paperback, School Supplies, Textbook and Instructional, Vertical File, and Video or DVD. Within each file, arrange the catalogs in alphabetical order by company name. When a new catalog is received, throw away the old one and replace it with the new one. Writing the date received shows you whether the catalog is current and helps when weeding the out-of-date ones.

Dorothy Pope, Lawrence County High School,
Lawrenceburg, Tennessee • January 2006

Top, Middle, or Bottom Shelf

To reshelve loads of books in a shorter amount of time, purchase a large two-sided book cart with three shelves on each side. Tell students to place their books on the cart in a special way after check-in: easy readers go on the top shelf, nonfiction books on the middle shelf, and the fiction and biography on the bottom. If one side fills before re-shelving, simply turn to the empty side. Students learn about call numbers, and shelving is quicker and easier!

Tammy Sauls, Mary Hughes School,
Piney Flats, Tennessee • January/February 2009

Use Every Inch of Space—Even the Windowsills!

Our library is housed in a building with incredibly deep windowsills. We realized that these windowsills, measuring 70 inches by 27 inches, would be a great way to solve our seating shortage if we could make them into window seats. Our maintenance department verified that the windows were permanently fastened and that the structure was sound to accept weight. With heavy-duty cushion foam from a craft store and inexpensive throw pillows and fabric, the unique reading areas cost only $40 per window seat. This was definitely less expensive than getting two library chairs, and the kids adore the "nook" aspect of the seats. You can even just pin the fabric around the cushion so that it is easy to remove and throw in the wash.

Courtney Lewis, Kirby Library, Wyoming Seminary Upper School, Kingston, Pennsylvania • March 2007

Check Out These Lights

Rotate unusual lights to brighten up your library. Test and purchase novelty lights at thrift stores and garage sales. Solicit lights from vendors who run contests such as magazine sales on your campus. Purchase strings of holiday lights such as Halloween bats and Valentine hearts when they go on sale after the holiday. Fake aquariums, lava lamps, LED speaker lights, night-lights, and medusa multi-armed lights can also be rotated in. Change the light about once a month for variety, and your light collection can last for years. Store them a in clear plastic shoe boxes to keep cords untangled.

Sheryl Kindle Fullner, Nooksack Valley Middle School, Everson, Washington • November/December 2008

Poster Ideas

ALA posters of celebrities with their favorite books are really popular in my library, as are the free posters available at conferences. Simply tacking posters up with thumbtacks damages them and can look cheap, but buying frames is way too expensive. Our solution is to have the posters dry-mounted onto a thick poster board at our local craft store. It costs only around $8 per poster (for a 22-inch by 36-inch poster) and is incredibly lightweight. Most craft stores will even attach a little metal hanger for you. Keep a stash of the mounted posters in the closet, and rotate them to keep the look of the library fresh.

Courtney Lewis, Kirby Library, Wyoming Seminary Upper School, Kingston, Pennsylvania • November/December 2006

A Clean Slate

Take *everything* down from your walls and put up new posters every few years. This sends a message to your staff that your library is about change and promotes new ideas. It is also a great way to think about what new messages you want to convey through the posters you select.

 Catherine Trinkle, Hickory Elementary, Avon, Indiana • February 2008

DISPLAYS AND BULLETIN BOARDS

Display Dummies

To highlight books in your collection, cover old hardcover books that are about to be weeded from your collection with brown paper bag covers. Search an online bookseller for the exact jacket of the new book(s) that you want to highlight. Print the covers on a color printer and then tape the covers to the brown paper covers. These book doubles are ready for the library display case, while the original books are available for circulation. When it is time to highlight different books, just take the color copy off the jacket and attach a new one.

 Diana Wendell, Dana L. West High School,
Port Byron, New York • August/September 2008

Organizing Décor

To get your monthly media-center decorations neatly organized without costing you a penny, gather 18 to 20 boxes with removable lids, such as empty copy-paper boxes. Set out 9 boxes, one for each month of the school year. As one box is filled, write the name of the month on the front of it, set it aside, and put an empty box in its place. Fill the boxes until all decorations have been separated by month. Create labels for each box in a word processing program using the following settings—page setup orientation: landscape; font: Times New Roman; font size: 150. Center the text on the page. Type each month's name, print the number of labels needed for each month, and tape the labels to the shorter end of the boxes.

Judi Wollenziehn, Bishop Miege High School,
Shawnee Mission, Kansas • April/May 2008

Return to Display

About two weeks before the end of each month, pull the seasonal books for the upcoming month. Put all items on reserve for a patron named "March LMC Display" when March is approaching, for example. Circulate the items as usual; however, when they are returned and scanned, they will cause an error message to appear. The message will state that the item is "reserved for March LMC Display." Your volunteers will know exactly where to put the book: back on the monthly student display.

Beverly Frett, Robert Clow Elementary,
Naperville, Illinois • January 2006

Fancy Lettering for Bulletin Boards, Signs, and More

1. Open Microsoft Word.

2. Open a new document.

3. Click on Insert on the toolbar at the top.

4. Next, click on Picture and then on Clip Art.

5. Click on Clips Online.

6. You will see a couple of search fields near the top right-hand corner. In the box next to it, type in one of the letters that you want (whatever patterns you see for that letter, you can assume will be there for every other letter).

7. Click on Go.

8. Click on the letter that you are interested in. It will open larger in a new browser window.

9. Click on Copy. If any dialogue boxes open up, I just click on Accept, Yes, and Okay (until it goes through the downloading of Active X and the permissions).

10. Once the downloading is complete, go back into your document in Word (by clicking on that file in your toolbar at the bottom of your screen) and click on Paste (or hold down the Ctrl and V buttons at the same time to paste).

11. You may resize the letter once you have it in Word.

12. Once you are happy with that one, go back to Clip Art and follow the same directions for each letter that you need.

13. Once you have chosen your style (by clicking on one letter), you may also click on the style number to see all the letters that look like that.

Have fun decorating!

Stacy Rosenthal, Upper Moreland Middle School, Hatboro, Pennsylvania, January 2007

Simple Flannel Board Solutions

Creating flannel board stories has never been easier! Simply open Microsoft Word, insert clip art images related to the characters and setting of the story, and size as needed. Print the images, cut them out, laminate them, and then attach a piece of self-adhesive felt to the back. Clip art images can also be used to create flannel board visuals for songs such as "The Bear Went Over the Mountain," "The Itsy Bitsy Spider," and many more.

 Malena Bisanti-Wall, American Heritage Academy, Canton, Georgia • January 2008

Shredded Paper on a Budget

Instead of buying multiple bags of expensive shredded paper in various colors, use colored butcher paper or construction paper. Run it through the school's paper shredder and use as needed.

 Aileen Kirkham, Decker Prairie Elementary School Library, Magnolia, Texas • January 2008

Stick 'Em Up

Use strong magnetic cup hooks or magnetic clamps to suspend garlands, lights, posters, pictures, dream catchers, and banners from metal door and window frames. This is superior to tape or other adhesives.

 Sheryl Kindle Fullner, Nooksack Valley Middle School, Everson, Washington • March/April 2009

One-Week Weeder

Once a week, haul all the books off one shelf in fiction and one in nonfiction, and put them on display. Move any books that look shabby or unloved or that are missing bar codes, spine labels, and so on into the to-do pile for that week. Select one book from the displayed books to be your favorite for when students ask. Display it on a cookbook rack or other fancy display stand with permanent words such as "Mrs. Fullner's Favorite." This ensures that by the end of the school year, you have personally handled every book and have not gotten into a rut as to which ones you promote.

Sheryl Kindle Fullner, Nooksack Valley Middle School, Everson, Washington • March 2007

Insights on Your Insides

To promote books on different medical conditions or accidents causing physical damage, suspend crutches, canes, and walking casts from the ceiling. The school nurse may have ones you can borrow. *Izzy, Willy-Nilly* (Simon Pulse, 2005) was a great excuse to hang up a jointed artificial leg that was very popular with students. Next year we will use the same garage sale prosthesis for Veterans Day or Team Able sports.

Sheryl Kindle Fullner, Nooksack Valley Middle School, Everson, Washington • May/June 2009

Bulletin Board Photo

Take a digital picture of your bulletin boards before you take them down and print it; tape the photo to the outside of the envelope where you store the letters and other decorations for the board. It will be easy to see in one glance the layout for the board the next time you need to put it up.

Tish Carpinelli, Lower Cape May Regional High School, Cape May, New Jersey • April/May 2007

Bulletin Board Themes

To decorate a bulletin board in the library, use a seasonal theme that also includes a library or reading slogan. Cut shapes out of extra book jackets to add a special touch to the bulletin board. For the winter holidays, cut triangle shapes from book jackets and create one large pine tree for the bulletin board. Cut heart shapes with a die-cut machine for February and create a pot overflowing with shamrock shapes for March.

In the spring, try blossom shapes with three-dimensional leaves from construction paper placed in a large brown flowerpot.

Janice Gumerman, Bingham Middle School,
Independence, Missouri • November/December 2006

Book Jacket Displays

If you don't have a lot of space to display books, use book jackets to display the different literary genres. On a bulletin board write down several genres such as fiction, science fiction, historical fiction, realistic fiction, and so on, and then glue book jackets next to each genre. Every few weeks, change the book jackets. It makes a really colorful bulletin board, and students will use it as a guide to locating books of their favorite genre.

Paty Perret Megerle, Ridgeview Elementary,
San Antonio, Texas • November/December 2006

Laminate Letters

Before you cut paper for bulletin board displays with a die-cut machine, always laminate the sheets first. This process helps keep the letters stiffer to stand up to reuse year after year.

Janice Gumerman, Bingham Middle School,
Independence, Missouri • November/December 2007

Organizing Bulletin Board Letters

We used to store bulletin board letters in a box, all sizes and colors in one jumble. Now we use plastic page protectors for each size and color and snap these into a three-ring binder. This takes very little room on the shelf and makes selection of letters easier; putting them away is easy, too—just grab the page with the color of letters you will be using and off you go!

Viola Lyons, Trinity College School, Port Hope, Ontario, October 2007

SUPPLIES

Down the Drain

Stationery stores carry fabulous graphic manila folders with wild designs. Use a discreet black metal dish drainer to hold a dozen of your most frequently used files upright and separated for easy access on your desk.

Sheryl Kindle Fullner, Nooksack Valley Middle School, Everson, Washington • August/September 2007

Super Tub of Fun

When students have creative projects for class, markers become a hot commodity. Knowing how easily art supplies can get misplaced, we bought an inexpensive clear plastic bin with a handle and dubbed it the "super tub of fun." It contains all the markers, crayons, glitter, glue, and stickers that we buy or collect throughout the year and is easily portable within the library. Our students enjoy asking for it, and everything stays together in one place.

Courtney Lewis, Kirby Library, Wyoming Seminary Upper School, Kingston, Pennsylvania • February 2007

Retaining the Original

When making numerous copies from a master, mark the original with "ORIGINAL" and the school year dates (e.g., "07–08") in yellow highlighter. The highlighter does not show up when you make new copies, but you always know that you are running low when you see this designation on a page in the folder where you keep the copies.

Janice Gumerman, Bingham Middle School, Independence, Missouri • October 2008

Library Duct Tape

When you receive a new school identification badge, cover it in book tape. The tape is clear and durable, and it protects the badge, delaying the return to the long line at Human Resources to get a replacement badge: *book tape, the duct tape of the library world.*

Kristi Y. Patton, Larkspur Middle School,
Virginia Beach, Virginia • October 2008

Wandering Scissors

Often teachers forget to take scissors to the workroom with them although they need to cut pages after laminating. Get some strong cord with wire in it and tie an old pair of scissors to the laminating machine with a long length of the cord. You won't lose scissors anymore.

Janice Gumerman, Bingham Middle School,
Independence, Missouri • February 2008

EQUIPMENT

End-of-Year Equipment Evaluations

At the end of the school year, just before the overhead projectors are returned, I distribute an equipment evaluation form to all staff and ask them to return it attached to their projector. I keep it very brief, including a choice of four boxes for them to check to describe how well they liked the machine and one box to check if the bulb needs replacing. I know that I don't need to look at a machine with the top rating, and I can also see which ones to examine more closely.

Tish Carpinelli, Lower Cape May Regional High School,
Cape May, New Jersey • April/May 2008

Equipment Purchases

Generate a basic list of classroom equipment/media with preferred vendors, brands, model numbers, and approximate prices. Keep this list on file for yourself and the school secretary for future ordering. This reduces the numbers of different bulbs and other accessories required for many different brands. You can select specific brands with a proven reliability factor too.

Aileen Kirkham, Decker Prairie Elementary School,
Magnolia, Texas • April/May 2008

Electrical Test

If you have a nonworking piece of equipment and are not sure whether it is broken or the problem is the electrical outlet, plug a handy night-light into the outlet to test it. This saves you from lugging around a lamp or other heavy equipment to check outlets.

Michelle Robertson, Park Elementary,
Tulsa, Oklahoma • October 2008

Equipment Reliability Factor

Use a silver or black permanent marker to write the arrival date on new equipment. This gives a timeline of durability when it breaks down and helps you to decide whether to reorder that brand of equipment again. If there's room on the equipment, write the date of any repairs too. Aesthetically it may not look pretty, but it's a practical way to maintain repair records and deter theft.

Aileen Kirkham, Decker Prairie Elementary School,
Magnolia, Texas • August / September 2008

Putting a Little WHITE on the Subject

Most TV monitors, DVD players, and VCRs have the "in" and "out" points clearly marked, but these markings are usually in the same color as the body of the device. Because I can't see the imprint that well, I brush a dab of correction fluid over the imprint. Now it is much easier to decipher the correct connection without having to move the equipment to better lighting!

Mary LaMar, Silver Lake (Kansas) Junior/Senior
High School • August / September 2008

Cutting the Cord

Do you have desktop computers that often get moved from one place to another? Make it hassle-free by always leaving power and Ethernet cords in place at both locations. Just pick up the computer and move it. You'll save a lot of time and avoid having to crawl around on the floor to find the right cord or plug.

Mary Alice Anderson, Winona (Minnesota) Area Public Schools • August/September 2006

Organizing Cables and Cords

To keep extra cables and cords organized, put comparable cables into large zippered freezer bags. Write on the bag what type of cable the bag contains. Keep all bags in a file cabinet drawer. This will keep your cables from tangling and let you know at a glance what cables you have. After organizing all the cables you can identify, take a digital picture of the mystery cables you cannot recognize, focusing on the end connectors. Send the photo in e-mail to all your teachers. Offer a prize (a chocolate bar is always popular!) to whoever can name the cable and its purpose.

Sarah C. Chase, Carroll Senior High School, Southlake, Texas • August/September 2006

Recycle and Reward

Two large office-supply chain stores allow certain toner and ink cartridges to be returned and recycled for a $3 merchandise credit. There are limits to how many may be returned or redeemed per day. Use the money collected from recycling to buy reading incentives or to reward library volunteers.

Sheryl Fullner, Nooksack Valley Middle School, Everson, Washington • February 2008

Mice Lockdown

To protect optical mice and computer cables from being stolen, secure them by placing a plastic self-locking tie around the connecting cables and part of the hardware on the back of the CPU unit. Students may still pull cables out of the CPU, but they will not be able to remove them without being detected.

 Laura Jeanette Brown, Paint Branch High School, Hanover, Maryland • January 2006

Those Pesky Overhead Projector Bulbs!

Our school has about six or seven different models of overhead projectors with, of course, unique bulbs for each one. Our teachers usually don't know what type of bulb belongs to their machine and often feel uncomfortable opening up their machine. So one of the librarians has to go to their classroom and inevitably brings the wrong bulb. We've solved this problem by simply attaching a piece of tape or a label on the back of the projector with the letter acronym for the bulb, so that teachers can immediately tell us which bulb to bring when they call from their classrooms. It saves us time and they are happier, faster!

 Courtney Lewis, Wyoming Seminary Upper School, Kingston, Pennsylvania • January 2007

Time to Laminate

Because we have two laminating machines in the teachers' workroom that take a specific amount of time to warm up, I have provided an inexpensive kitchen timer for the teachers' workroom. This provides a reminder that the machines are ready when the timer rings. It also keeps the machines from being on for hours on end while someone waits for them to warm up to the appropriate temperature.

 Janice Gumerman, Bingham Middle School, Independence, Missouri • January 2008

It's a Shoe-In!

To organize all of your remotes, buy a few plastic hanging shoe trees and label each pocket with the corresponding TV or projector unit name and color.

Jennifer Alevy, Sara Poinier, and Judy Larson, Horizon High School, Thornton, Colorado • January/February 2009

Oh, That One's Grumpy!

Name and color-code all of your equipment. For example, we have seven TV/DVD/VCR units; we named them after the Seven Dwarves and gave each a color and a picture of a dwarf, which we taped on the side of the unit. Paint the top of the corresponding remotes to match the unit.

Jennifer Alevy, Sara Poinier, and Judy Larson, Horizon High School, Thornton, Colorado • January/February 2009

Emergency Lighting

If your district is subject to occasional abrupt power outages during storms without supplementary or emergency lighting, solicit an LED lantern from your PTA, VFW, or other charitable group. The lanterns crank to replenish the battery, and the five to seven LED lights provide a safe level of illumination to continue manual jobs for staff or to facilitate evacuation of student groups. One lantern placed up high does much to diminish mayhem. The lanterns provide about five times the amount of light as a similar flashlight, and they illuminate a much larger radius.

Sheryl Kindle Fullner, Nooksack Valley Middle School, Everson, Washington • January/February 2009

In the Dark

For emergency checkout when the computers are down, have several clipboards prepared with boxes for student checkout information, including first and last name, student number, title of book, and bar code. Boxes are better than lines because they keep all the information contained instead of straggling down the page. Multiple boards speed up the checkouts. In case of power outages, store a windup flashlight with the boards.

Sheryl Kindle Fullner, Nooksack Valley Middle School, Everson, Washington • March/April 2009

Headphone Keepers

In order to help keep headphones and their wires in order, attach plastic self-stick hooks to the sides of the monitors. Then train the students to take off the headphones and replace them on the mounted hooks after use to keep the wires from getting tangled. Works like a dream. Headphones are easily visible at a glance, so you can account for every headphone.

Janice Gumerman, Bingham Middle School, Independence, Missouri • March 2008

Tracking Equipment

To keep track of all of your equipment, use a whiteboard hanging by your equipment room. Create rows for each piece of equipment and columns for who checked items out, what equipment she took, and if she took any other supplementary equipment, such as Ethernet cords, extension cords, and so on. Color-code everything. We use erasable markers for the board and clean it off at the end of every day. Teachers sign up for equipment in advance on a sign-up sheet next to the whiteboard.

Jennifer Alevy, Sara Poinier, and Judy Larson, Horizon High School, Thornton, Colorado • November/December 2008

Bag Those Remotes and Cables

Keep DVD remote controls and RCA cables together in resealable bags so that everything is traceable when these devices are checked out of the library for classroom use.

Janice Gumerman, Bingham Middle School, Independence, Missouri • October 2007

Bar-Code Remotes

If you have DVD players for checkout, it is easier to label and bar-code the remotes than to label the machines themselves. Simply pull the remote out of a drawer and scan it. This helps to keep teachers accountable for the remotes that tend to get misplaced easily.

Janice Gumerman, Bingham Middle School, Independence, Missouri • October 2007

Input/Output

Most VCRs have more than one input choice. When transferring from a mini-DV camcorder to a full-size VHS tape, it is necessary to select the correct input on the VCR in order to transfer the video. Even if you are able to view the pictures on your TV screen, the transfer may not be made if you have not made the correct input choice. Check your VCR instruction manual and the remote to identify the proper plugs and proper input choice.

Cheryl Youse, J. L. Lomax Elementary School, Valdosta, Georgia • October 2007

ACQUISITIONS

Learn Before Buying

Do you want more information about a DVD or book? Check the company's Web site for the specific program you are reviewing. If the Web site is not listed in your material, search for more information using the name of the producer, distributor, or title. On these other sites you usually find a more detailed description than can be included in a review. These descriptions often include a preview of the program and teaching materials. For books you can often locate the author's home page and learn more there.

 Anitra Gordon, Ann Arbor, Michigan • October 2008

Free Entertainment Videos and DVDs

Be alert to video stores that are going out of business. Some owners will donate VHS tapes and DVDs to schools as a tax write-off. Our school has a sizable entertainment video collection thanks to two local video store owners who allowed me to come and choose from their selection before their final sell-off. These are mostly movies on which I would not have spent money from my budget, but they are enjoyable leisure viewing for students and staff.

 Tish Carpinelli, Lower Cape May Regional High School, Cape May, New Jersey • February 2008

PROCESSING BOOKS AND MATERIALS

Checking Out Sets and Unusual Items

To circulate sets and unusual items, create laminated blank, bar-coded index cards. Take an 8 by 5-inch index card and cut it in half. On the non-lined side place a bar code on the center bottom and write "Title" with a line above the word. On the lined side put a line with "Sign Here" underneath it. Laminate these cards, punch a hole in the top middle, and hang them on a hook near the circulation desk. When someone wants to check out a set of markers or a set of class novels, write the title, cost, and—if a set of individual units—how many items in the group (e.g., class set of *Animal Farm*—32 books). Then have the person checking the item(s) out sign the lined side. In the computer scan the bar code and enter it as a temporary bar code with all the pertinent information. Then place the cards on another hook close to the first one. When the items come in, you will be able to quickly find the bar-coded index card, scan it in, wipe off the laminated card with a damp cloth, and reuse the card. Because you entered the information in the computer as a temporary item, you can print out overdue and fine slips.

Anna Brueher, Silver Stage High School,
Silver Springs, Nevada • January 2007

Book Hospital

During busy check-in time, you need a strategy for handling damaged books to expedite the check-in process. Before a book is scanned in, look over the book to check its condition. When damage is found, slip in a laminated bookmark at the point of damage to indicate the problem. The individual strips may say, for example, *page torn, ink, spine, stain, cover, wrinkled, pencil,* and *other.* Set the book aside in an appropriately decorated "Book Hospital" box so that check-in can proceed. For minor damage, remove the book from the student record. More serious damage warrants a fine, so don't check in the book, and wait to generate a fine letter during a less busy time. Once a week, make all repairs.

Pat Miller, Sue Creech Elementary,
Katy, Texas • January 2007

Bag Those Bits and Bytes

When I circulate small items that cannot be labeled or bar-coded, I put these in a resealable plastic sandwich-sized baggie. Then I attach the bar code to the outside of the baggie and scan that for checkout. This works well for such items as memory cards, wireless presentation devices, and flash drives. And best of all, it helps me keep track of these for inventory and end-of-year returns.

Janice Gumerman, Bingham Middle School,
Independence, Missouri • May/June 2009

One-Stop Sorting

Create "library action slips" (four quarter-pages fit well on 8½ by 11-inch paper) with a list of the most common clerical to-do items and copy them onto bright paper. Keep them handy at the circulation desk, and then just check the action needed, such as "new bar code," "new spine label," "glue/tape spine," or "reserve book for _____." Insert the action slip into the book until you have time to attend to the fixes.

Amy Linden, Bear River High School,
Grass Valley, California • May/June 2009

Manual Checkout

Sometimes you need to run a manual checkout because of problems with your circulation software. Instead of writing down the student's name and the book bar code, make a computer spreadsheet with one column for the student's name and one column for the book barcode. If your students have IDs with barcodes, this works easily. Most scanners still work even when not in the circulation software. When the books are returned, it is easy to find the bar code in the listing by using the Find function and scanning in the barcode for the book. If you have to do this for more than one day, you can easily start another spreadsheet so that you can keep your due dates straight.

Nancy LeCrone, Rockwall-Heath High School,
Heath, Texas • November/December 2006

SECTION 2:

WORKING
WITH STUDENTS
IN THE
LIBRARY

The ideal elementary library is teeming with eager, inquisitive readers and researchers. They come in classes, in small groups, and on their own to the heart of their school, the media center. The library staff learns the names and preferences of the many young patrons as they teach, facilitate, and collaborate with 21st-century learners. Carefully taught and learned expectations and procedures for conducting business and learning in the library make the library the "Shangri-La" of the school. Smooth sailing is ahead once the proper procedures are established for book checkout and care, computer use, and all the nitty-gritty aspects of a well-oiled library machine.

Tips in this section are divided into the following topics:

- Student Behavior
- Checking Books and Materials
- Overdue and Lost Books

STUDENT BEHAVIOR

Not-So-Hidden Picture Books

Our collection of "puzzle books" is kept in the library, and these books do not circulate. Leave "I Spy" and "Where's Waldo?" books on the magazine rack for browsing by students who have finished checking out. They love to look through the pages and find all the hidden pictures.

Gayle Stein, Central Avenue School,
Madison, New Jersey • April/May 2008

Reading Buddies

A great way to encourage kindergarteners to become good library citizens is to reward them with the privilege of "checking out" a reading buddy for the week. We keep a variety of stuffed animals available in a reading buddy chest, from fluffy bunnies to cuddly book characters such as the Cat in the Hat. We also keep a book bag for each of our three kindergarten classes. Each week at the end of library class, a student who has displayed proper library etiquette—that is, who was a good listener during story time, who used a quiet voice when looking for a book, who was courteous to other classmates, and who returned her book from the previous week—is selected to take home the reading buddy. The proud student leaves the library with his selected book and reading buddy in its own special book bag. Tip: to avoid confusion over which class has returned its reading buddy and which has not, make sure to bar-code the book bag and check it out to the student at the same time he checks out his book.

Kathy Greenfield, Covenant Day School,
Matthews, North Carolina • October 2008

Not on My Shelf!

At the beginning of each school year in our K–6 school, I have students in the second through sixth grades "adopt" a shelf of their own. The shelves have colorful stickers with the owners' names, and the students are responsible for helping to keep their shelves organized by call numbers. The students sign a contract with me promising to keep their shelf organized. This encourages them to visit the library to check on their shelves, teaches them about library organization, and helps them develop a real interest in their school library. They often check out books when they visit and begin to view the library as a friendly place that they enjoy visiting.

Marjorie Shuster, Hebrew Academy of Nassau County,
West Hempstead, New York • August/September 2008

The ABCs of Place Markers

If you ask your young students to use rulers or some other type of place marker when they pull books from the shelves, use a label maker and attach a label to this place marker that includes the alphabet. This way, students have the alphabet right in front of them to help them navigate the shelves of books.

Denise Dragash, Prairie Trace Elementary,
Carmel, Indiana • February 2008

No Child Left

Sometimes librarians are responsible for teaching students how to use a mouse, a scanner, or other device that demands small motor coordination. To remind yourself how difficult this is for some beginners, use your own non-dominant hand: if you are right-handed, try it with your left.

Sheryl Fullner, Nooksack Valley Middle School,
Everson, Washington • January 2008

Sneak Peeks

For younger students who are learning about authors and illustrators, tell them to look for a "sneak peek" on the inside back cover. There they might find a picture and short biography of the person(s) who wrote the story and drew the pictures. The children love seeing these photos!

Margie Sawyer, Assumption Catholic School,
Bellingham, Washington • January 2008

Post-Novel Activity

After reading a novel as a class, ask students to write down three questions they'd like to ask the book's author. Have students exchange papers and answer the questions as if they were the author. Read the questions and answers aloud for discussion.

Claudette Hegel,
Bloomington, Minnesota • January/February 2009

Time Fillers

If you have a few minutes of class time to fill before breaks or dismissal, ask students to find an object in the room or outside the windows that seems to include a letter of the alphabet. Do the branches of the tree form a letter *A*? Is the doorknob an *O*?

Claudette Hegel,
Bloomington, Minnesota • March/April 2009

Topic Bingo

You can make bingo games for nearly any subject by creating cards with answers to questions. For example, entries for math can be answers to equations, and entries for vocabulary can be answers to the meaning of the words. A few other topics could be state capitals, presidents, and Civil War facts (generals, battles, and other topics). Making the game can be time-consuming, but it can be used over and over.

Claudette Hegel,
Bloomington, Minnesota • March/April 2009

Alphabet Facts

After studying a specific subject or book, ask students to think of a fact about the subject corresponding to each letter of the alphabet. For example, if the subject is "Abraham Lincoln," the letter *A* could correspond to his first name, the letter *B* to his birthday is February 12, and so on.

Claudette Hegel,
Bloomington, Minnesota • November/December 2008

Everyday Math

A way to combine math and everyday life lessons is to determine how much something costs for a year. For example, calculate how much food a pet eats, how many servings are in a bag or can, and the cost of the product to determine annual cost. Comparing the costs of canned food and dry food or the cost for a big dog versus a small dog or a cat versus a dog will provide even more learning opportunities.

Claudette Hegel,
Bloomington, Minnesota • November/December 2008

Library Mystery Bag

Explaining library rules is a necessary but often boring part of library instruction. It's lots of fun, though, with the "Library Mystery Bag." Decorate a bag on the outside (or buy one) with pictures of books or detectives. Place objects in it related to library rules or behavior or care of books. Examples are a bar of soap (clean hands); a dog bone and baby rattle (keep books away from pets and younger siblings); a clear bag containing a torn, dirty book and a new, clean book (caring for books); or your smiling picture (you are happy to have kids in the library). Choose one student to cover her eyes, reach in, and pull out an object, while the rest of the kids guess how the object is related to library rules. We finish by listing all the rules and posting them in the library.

Shelley Riskin, Pleasant Ridge School,
Glenview, Illinois • November/December 2006

Do It Yourself

When students stop by while I have a class in session and cannot help them, I have them fill out a self-checkout slip. Students take the slip, put their name and their teacher's name on it, and place the slip in the book, which they then leave on my counter. When I am finished with my class, I check the books out to those students on the slips and deliver the books before the end of the day. The students get to check out the books they want at any time, and I don't have to worry about interruptions.

Leslie Williams, California (Missouri) Elementary
• November/December 2007

What's That Treasure?

Keeping intriguing items on the circulation desk makes the library an interesting place. Hide small, themed treasures in empty water bottles filled with colored rice or bird seed. Treasures can be purchased at hobby or craft shops. Use letter cubes, plastic animals, coins, or buttons of bright colors. Create themes to match Dewey decimal system subjects. This makes a great door prize giveaway for professional meetings as well.

Lisa Hunt, Apple Creek Elementary,
Moore, Oklahoma • May/June 2009

Nursery Rhymes

To add a little fun to a nursery rhyme theme, have a student or students act out the rhyme and then interview them. For example, for Old King Cole, one student sits on the throne as we recite the rhyme. Then we ask Old King Cole some questions about what it is like to be king. Continue with other rhymes. For example, I asked one student, the Old Woman from the Shoe, "How is it in there?" and she said, "Pretty stinky!" You will laugh at the impromptu answers.

Lenore Piccoli, Mount Pleasant Elementary School,
Livingston, New Jersey • October 2007

Long Lines at the "Checkout Counter"?

As efficient as we are, our primary students find they sometimes have to wait a bit to get their books checked out. Solution? I put easy-to-read comics on the side of the library circulation computer: *Dennis the Menace, Mutts,* and sometimes *Garfield.* I find the older students will read to the younger ones, and the kids often remind me that it's time to put up new ones. The cartoons help the children wait responsibly and practice reading at the same time!

Melinda Stucker, Mount Lebanon School,
West Lebanon, New Hampshire • October 2007

CHECKING BOOKS AND MATERIALS

Homemade Library Cards

Make library cards for your students to use when checking out books. Just print out the bar code and the child's name, paste each bar code onto a piece of card stock (about the size of a library card), and then laminate it. Allowing students to use their cards at the media center and to scan the book they are checking out gives each child ownership of the book. They are more likely to return the book on their next visit, just so that they can use their card and the scanner again.

Susan Jolly, Lincoln Elementary,
Waterloo, Iowa • April/May 2007

Contain the Cards

Use a small plastic supermarket container for each class's library cards. Write the teacher's name and grade on the top and sides of the container with permanent marker. For checkout, spread out the cards on a table, or the student can shuffle through the container and find his own card. After individual or group checkout, return the cards to the container and place it on a shelf for easy location. Students won't lose cards, and the teachers will be pleased to be without them.

Sheila Klaassen, Bursley Elementary School,
Grand Rapids, Michigan • April/May 2008

"I Trust You" Books

There are times when students might not be able to check out library materials because they have too many books out, have overdue books, or owe fines or for some other reason. Make uncataloged paperbacks available for these students in a collection called "I Trust You" books. To the kids I explain, "I trust you" to return these books when you are finished reading them. Because they aren't cataloged, I don't really track them, but the kids respect that, and the books come back. You can build this type of collection from book-fair and reading-club rewards, but donations of books that are high-interest and in good condition are also useful. Label the books "I Trust You" on the cover for ease of shelving.

Tracy A. Fitzwater, Crescent School District,
Joyce, Washington • October 2008

Promoting via Automation

Instead of listing a grade level in the library patron module, put the student's graduation year. This makes it easy to roll over records from year to year without having to edit each individual student. For example, third grade might be 2017.

Nooksack District Librarians,
Nooksack, Washington • January 2008

Shelf Marker/Library Card

If you are on a tight budget, do not purchase library cards/identification cards for students. Combine shelf markers with library cards. Use your circulation program to print out patron bar codes. Adhere them to a 2 by 6-inch piece of poster board. Let the students decorate them, and then you can laminate them. The cards can be color-coded by grade level and sorted by class in a small filing box at the front of the library. Now the students grab their library cards as soon as they enter the library for checkout and use them along the way to mark shelf spaces so that the books are placed back in order.

Bobby Riley, H. O. Wheeler Elementary School, Burlington, Vermont • January/February 2009

It's in the Bag!

For kindergarten classes, purchase a quantity of plastic drawstring bags from a library supply vendor. Then attach a student name and bar-code label directly to the bag. Kindergartners keep their library media-center books in these bags to carry to and from school and the library media center. When they are ready to check out, they place their books in the plastic bag and bring them to the counter. Then simply scan the bar code on the bag. and scan the bar codes of the books in the bag. This has really helped keep these little ones organized. Parents know to look for this bag and to keep library media-center books together in the bag as well.

Janice Gumerman, Bingham Middle School, Independence, Missouri, October 2006

OVERDUE AND LOST BOOKS

That Was Easy!

We encourage our middle school students to renew their books when they are due, if the item is still needed. We also encourage them to renew before a fine occurs on the item. At the start of the school year, I put an Easy Button at the front desk. (You may recognize this item from the Staples office-supply commercials and can purchase one there.) The students ask why it is there. I answer, "When you renew a book, *and* there is *not* a late fine, you may push the easy button." They respond with, "That was easy." They are thrilled. The button makes a slight noise, but it is good for smiles, and the positive reinforcement has paid off. Now the students ask to push the easy button when they renew. We're ahead of last year on renewals, and we've had a lot of smiles!

Tricia Baackes, Steffen Middle School,
Mequon, Wisconsin • April/May 2008

Making Book Return Easy

To help get students to return books, buy an "Easy Button"—one that you press to hear it say, "That was easy." Let the students push the Easy Button only if they return their books. I get smiles, giggles, and big, big laughs! Everyone wants to push the Easy Button, and everyone is bringing books back!

Suzanne Hooper, Riverview Elementary School,
Kings Canyon Unified School District, California • March 2008

Encourage Book Returns!

If students can't check out a new book because they have overdue books, a "Save Box" allows students to choose one book they really want. Have them fill out a note-sized paper with their name and classroom. Stamp the next due date on the note and slip it into the book's pocket. Finally, put their book in the "Save Box" (we use a milk crate placed near the checkout desk). We hold the book for a week. If students forget to come for their books, the stamped date will help you remember to put the book back in circulation. You and the students will be surprised how this incentive helps children become more responsible library users!

Melinda Stucker, Mt. Lebanon School, West Lebanon, New Hampshire, January 2008

Refund Policy Revisited

Instead of automatically processing a refund for the return of a lost book, generate a form to find out whether the parent prefers a refund. You'd be surprised at how many will donate the dollars to buy more books. Keep the signed form on file as documentation of the parent's response.

Here is a sample:

(Date)

Dear Family of (Child's Name),

Refund Notice

Your child returned his/her lost book that was paid for by you. Please return this form and check your preference.

_____ I prefer to have a full refund sent to me.

_____ I would like for my previous payment to serve as a donation to my child's library.

Parent Signature _____

_____

Aileen Kirkham, Decker Prairie Elementary School Library, Magnolia, Texas, October 2008

When They Forget Their Library Books

When students forget to return their books, I let them go ahead and select books that I save for them. We have a shelf behind the circulation desk where these titles are put aside for three days. The kids use their time in the same way as their classmates who have remembered to return their materials. It also gives the children an incentive to bring their books to the library before the next class.

Gayle Stein, Central Avenue School,
Madison, New Jersey • August/September 2008

R.O.B.O.T. Award Idea

In an effort to encourage book return in a timely manner, present classes that return all of their library books with a R.O.B.O.T. (Returned Our Books on Time) Award. It can be a sign for the classroom door, a "real" traveling stand-up robot, or any other eye-catching robot to pass out to each class as they R.O.B.O.T.!

Leslie Ashby, Hudson Independent School District,
Lufkin, Texas • February 2007

The Return of the Bookworms

Try a visual reminder to help kindergarteners return books on time. Put up a "We Are Good Bookworms in Kindergarten. We Bring Our Books Back on Time!" sign, using a different colored bookworm face for each class. Every week, students who bring their book back earn a link for their class's bookworm chain, and each class in which all books are returned on time earns five bonus links. Then you can host a celebration party for the class with the longest bookworm.

Leslie Williams, California (Missouri) Elementary School
• March/April 2009

Stamp a Bookmark

Cut out bookmarks from white scrap paper and hand them out to each primary-grade student on the first day of class. Each week, choose a stamp of a literary character or animal. Also, try to tie in stamps that relate to holidays or celebrations. When the students line up to return their library books, put the stamp on the bookmark. If you can, use different colored ink each week. The students love to collect as many stamps as possible. They reuse the same bookmark until both sides are filled. Then they receive a new blank bookmark. Only students who return their books get a stamp. This encourages them to remember to bring in their library books on time.

Esther Peck, Wemrock Brook School,
Manalapan, New Jersey • March 2007

Book Return

To promote timely book return for kindergarten students, utilize a "Race to Return" in which each kindergarten class has a small racetrack displayed on the circulation desk. Each time all students in a class return their books on time, the class earns a racecar on its track. When five racecars are earned, the students have a "party" at the end of the next library class, where they are given a special treat. Other visual display ideas besides cars on a racetrack include paper spaceships in outer space, spiders on a web, or library books on a shelf.

 Rebecca Raub, Canon-McMillan School District,
Canonsburg, Pennsylvania • October 2007

TEACHING
LIBRARY
SKILLS

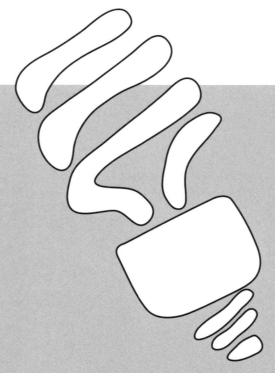

Although the job of teaching the skills necessary to develop successful 21st-century learners is a school-wide goal, the school librarian takes a leadership role in this endeavor. At the heart of this role, the librarian is teacher. He opens the child's eyes to the world of information and helps feed his natural curiosity.

Making the library an inclusive and comfortable setting where all students find success is just a fraction of the library media specialist's goals. Teaching students in ways that make them able to transfer the skills they learn in the library to other settings in another goal. These important skills will become the basis for lifelong learning and information literacy as students gather, process, evaluate, and repackage information throughout their lives.

Tips in this section are divided into the following topics:

- Book Basics
- Dewey Decimal System
- Finding Books
- Research

BOOK BASICS

Organizing by Genre

To reinforce lessons on genres, place the names of genres and pictures depicting the genres on the tables in the library. For example, use a unicorn picture for fantasy on one table, a covered wagon for historical fiction, a picture of a man with a magnifying glass for mystery, and so on. Have the students line up at the end of their library lesson and describe for them the characteristics of a specific genre. When they recognize the genre, have the students gather around the table at which the genre is represented. As the year goes on, change this up a little by giving examples of titles of series or authors who write certain genres.

Diane P. Smithson, Old Donation Center,
Virginia Beach, Virginia • August/September 2008

Reference Mnemonic

Do your students have a hard time remembering what each reference book does?

Here is a mnemonic that the kids find helpful:

Dictionary—Defines
Encyclopedia—Explains
Thesaurus—The same
Almanac—All Main Facts
Where It's At—Atlas

Rhonda Sobecki, Jackson Elementary,
Colorado Springs, Colorado • October 2007

The Author in the Dell

My kindergarten, first grade, and second grade students often get the concept of author and illustrator mixed up, so I created a solution. We sing, "The author writes the words; the author writes the words; that's how the book is made; the author writes the words" to the tune of "The Farmer in the Dell." Now all the students remember what an author does.

Linda Tuck, Glen Burnie (Maryland) Park Elementary
• April/May 2007

DEWEY DECIMAL SYSTEM

Hide and Go Seek

While introducing each section of the Dewey decimal system to third through fifth graders, use a prop. In our case, it is a large wooden tiger we have named "Tigger." Tigger sits on the shelf in the area I want them to explore that day. After describing and showing examples of the types of books in that classification area, I ask students to "go find Tigger" during checkout time. They are encouraged to browse and check out a book from that section. Tigger helps out when a class project requires students to use a certain area. For example, he sits on top of the biographies or the world history area when students are looking for books for research. During Poetry Month, he hangs out in the poetry shelves. When he is not "working" in a particular section, Tigger enjoys a prominent spot where everyone can see him and serves as a great helper when it comes time to find a certain handout or form that needs to be picked up. Stuffed animals or other props displayed around the library can help point out the beginning of the alphabet in a section or a particular spot to start lining up after class. For example, "The ape shows us the letter A" or "Line up next to Clifford."

 Holly Cobb, Shady Lane Elementary,
Menomonee Falls, Wisconsin • April/May 2007

Dewey Dilemma Game Using Book Jacket Covers

Collect about 20 nonfiction book jacket covers. Divide the class into teams—usually four members to a team. Give each student a copy of the Dewey decimal chart that has the numbers and descriptions of what types of books are found in each section. Each team takes a turn. Hold up a jacket cover and ask team members to confer with one another until they reach a consensus as to what section that book would fit into. I usually require that they tell me the general area rather than an exact number, but you could make it harder by asking for more specific answers. If they are right, hand them the jacket cover; if they are wrong, go to the next team until you get a correct answer. Discuss why their answer was right. The team with the most book jackets covers at the end wins prizes.

Carol Crawford, Fort Lewis Elementary, Northside
Middle School, Roanoke, Virginia • April/May 2007

Personalized Shelf Markers

To personalize a Dewey decimal lesson for second and third graders, use plastic shelf markers, paint sticks, or other materials, such as the ends of mini-blinds. Each week, the students find their shelf markers at their assigned tables and know it's time to talk Dewey. As you introduce new sections of the nonfiction area, the students place stickers of their favorite Dewey Decimal subject areas on the far end of their shelf markers. Create these stickers with a picture and the Dewey call number in a word processing program and print them on sticker paper. Volunteers can create and cut up the Dewey stickers. Personalized shelf markers travel around with the students as they shop for books. Students can also take them to the OPAC station as they search the catalog. Using sticky notes and pencils at the OPAC machines, students can stick the call number sticky note on their stick as they walk through the stacks locating the book. Students place the shelf markers in a labeled can at the circulation desk as they grab their library card to check out.

Krissy Neddo, Pashley Elementary Library,
Glenville, New York • October 2008

Dewey Races

During a unit on shelving nonfiction books, students participate in Dewey Races. Create small, replica book spines out of paper by drawing a slim rectangular box in a word processing program and typing in all required information (title, author, Dewey call number). Print and cut out a set for each student or team. Students then race to put their "books" in order. It can be taken a step further: students can replicate an actual shelf using the paper spines and check their answers by going around the library to find their "shelf" and compare it to the actual one. This is a great way to involve kinesthetic learners in a library lesson.

Rebecca Raub, Canon-McMillan School District, Canonsburg, Pennsylvania, February 2008

The Dewey Decimal System and Who Cares?

To help students understand the subject arrangement of nonfiction books, have some books from each classification (one classification at a time) on display by the order of the numbers, such as 100s the first time, then the 200s, and so on. In addition, put the poster for that category with the books. Change the display every two weeks. Allow students to check out these books and find replacements to continue through an entire two-week period with that number range. Hand out Dewey decimal bookmarks so that students can see what subjects will be coming up. Periodically make a school-wide announcement to highlight each of the categories and maintain interest in reading from these sections.

Sharon Thomas, Myers Middle School, Savannah, Georgia • March 2007

Adopt-a-Shelf

Create an Adopt-a-Shelf program to entice students to help out in the library. With the Adopt-a-Shelf program, a student selects or adopts a particular shelf in the library that he or she will be responsible for maintaining, including shelf reading, shelving, and displaying books. A label is placed on that shelf that says, "This shelf is maintained by [name of student]." Students are then given basic training on the Dewey decimal system and how to shelve books properly.

 Mary L. Knopp, Academy of Mount St. Ursula, Bronx, New York • May/June 2009

FINDING BOOKS

Pre-Searches

To keep from having to do a catalog search each time a student asks a common question, I searched all the common subjects—for example, love stories, baseball, science fiction, relationships, and so on. I also included pertinent history subjects from which the students can choose a book for a history/social studies book report (e.g. World War I, the Depression, prejudice, Vietnam, etc.). I alphabetized all these search results into a notebook and put each sheet into a sheet protector. Now students can just take the sheet out of the notebook and look for books on those topics. I update the pages in the book annually to make sure the collection additions are included in the lists. I print out new lists and add them to the notebook when new common questions arise.

Frances Hazelwood, Fuqua School,
Farmville, Virginia • October 2008

Practice Shelving

To give students practice shelving books and to help them understand how books are arranged, use the extra spine label stickers that come with your book orders. Stick them on to colored paper and laminate the squares. Also make some paper "shelves" on which to arrange the "books." Teach students how to notice if the book is fiction or nonfiction and how to then place their "books" on the "shelf" in order.

Jennifer Manstrom, Wyndmere (North Dakota)
Public School • August/September 2007

Clip-Art Shelf Helpers

In first and second grade it is difficult for students to locate books on the easy nonfiction shelves using the Dewey number. To help the children find their way to their favorite nonfiction subjects, use small clip-art pictures. Laminate the pictures and then attach them under the corresponding subject (i.e., cats, football, dinosaurs, etc.). Our students have become much more independent and find their favorites quite easily.

 Sherry Holler, Limerick (Pennsylvania) Elementary
• January 2007

Library Four Corners

Do your students still ask you where the fiction section is or where to find a book when the catalog tells them it's at 398.2? This game gets students better acquainted with the library than library tours do. To play, designate four places at which students can stand (the "corners") that are close to each of these sections: fiction, nonfiction, everybody, and reference. When you say "go," students quickly move to the corner of their choice. After 10 seconds, say "stop." Students still moving must go to the closest corner. Then hold up a book that is obviously from one of those corners (take these books from a box so that nobody can see what's coming next) and have students identify the area in which it would be found. Students standing in that corner sit down. Continue until only one student is left. That child gets to check out an extra book or gets to be the go/stop caller for the next game. Involve the teacher by having her show the books and act as the noise police—students who talk automatically have to sit down.

 Pat Miller, Sue Creech Elementary,
Katy, Texas • March 2006

More Uses for Book Jackets

Use a file of book jackets or pictures of books from displays to help students learn to use the catalog system and find books independently.

After you model computer and shelf searches, students pick a book jacket and then look up the title, author, and subject on the catalog system. They jot down the call number and go find the book (if the catalog shows it to be available) that matches the cover. Require fiction, easy fiction, and nonfiction searches. If a child wants to check out the book that day, take the book jacket out of the bin so that students can find books that are actually on the shelves.

Mary Louise Sanchez,
Thornton, Colorado • March 2006

Aisles of Books

Primary students have difficulty finding books on their own and don't understand Dewey decimal numbers. Explain that the library media center is like a supermarket. Just as items are placed in certain sections of the supermarket (e.g., cereals, frozen foods, dairy), books are placed in specific places in the library media center. Label the floor between bookshelves or the ends of each bookcase with giant numbers and letters as if they were aisles in the supermarket. Cut out 1A and 1B and laminate them. Place them on the first row of the nonfiction side. Continue with 2A and 2B and consecutive numbers for each additional aisle. When a student needs a dinosaur book, I say, "Look down Aisle 2B." For the fiction section, place giant letters on the floor or on the ends of the fiction bookcases. Now young students can "shop" independently in the aisles for their library media center books!

Esther Peck, Wemrock Brook School,
Manalapan, New Jersey • October 2006

RESEARCH

Quality Questioning

To move students to higher-order thinking, try asking more "why" questions and fewer "what" questions. For example, ask them, "Why do you think bears hibernate?" rather than "What do bears do during the winter?" Students are less likely to copy and paste answers from the Web if they have to provide rationale rather than simply regurgitate facts.

Donna Miller, Mesa County Valley School District 51, Grand Junction, Colorado • August/September 2006

Quality Questioning #2: Everyone Is on the Hook!

So many times when we ask questions, the same students respond, so we really do not have an opportunity to assess whether all students in the library are engaged and learning. To prevent this situation, tell the students that when you ask a question, you want no hands raised, but that you will select someone to answer the question. When students are uncertain about who you will call on to answer a question, they *all* tend to pay attention.

Donna Miller, Mesa County Valley School District 51, Grand Junction, Colorado • February 2007

Quality Questioning #3: Five "Why's"

To get students to think on a deeper level about various topics, ask "why" five times after you ask an initial question. The initial question could be one that requires a factual answer, and then you probe with five "why's" to get additional information and move students to critical thinking. Example: "What do bears do in the winter?" Answer: "They hibernate." Question: "Why do you think they hibernate?" Answer: "Because food sources are scarce in the winter." Question: "Why are food sources scarce?" Answer: "Because much of the vegetation dies." Question: "Why does vegetation die in the winter?" And so on.

 Donna Miller, Mesa County Valley School District 51, Grand Junction, Colorado • February 2007

WORKING WITH TEACHERS

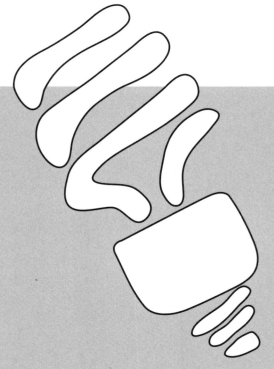

Establishing a positive working relationship with the teachers in the school is a vital precursor to building collaboration with staff. Seeking input from teachers is one step to help the librarian in selecting resources congruent to the curriculum and school goals. Collaborating together, the teacher and librarian can identify specific student and school goals and match materials to meet those needs. Student learning skyrockets when teachers and the librarian collaborate to present dynamic and meaningful lessons and units.

The tips in this section include the following:

- Attracting Teachers to the Library
- Promoting Library Materials
- Working Together
- Teaching Together

ATTRACTING TEACHERS TO THE LIBRARY

The Way to Their Hearts

To show teachers your new books, throw a "Breakfast with Books" after each new shipment arrives. Offer bagels, coffee, and fruit, and display all the books you have just received. This is a great way to feed the staff and get them into the library—they love it, and the books get used!

Tara LaCerra, Westmoor Elementary School, Northbrook, Illinois • February 2007

Time Together

To make your library more inviting for teachers and staff, block off a time of "no classes" during lunchtime each day so that they can come in to eat, browse for books, and just chat with you and their colleagues. Provide coffee, tea, sweets (particularly chocolates), and other snacks to keep them coming. During book fairs, set up a special table to allow teachers and staff a place to eat in the book-laden library. Book fair sales will zoom as they come in, enjoy the new books, and put aside stacks of items they plan to purchase before the fair ends. This time together during the busy day allows all educators to maintain a good working relationship with each other.

Linda Mitchell, Indian Valley Elementary School, Floyd County (Virginia) Public Schools • April/May 2007

Start the Day Right

Host an annual "Breakfast with Books" to showcase your major purchases. Show off your ordering skills when you invite the administrative team along with your staff. Make signs for picture books, fiction, professional books, poetry, nonfiction, and featured authors. Serve pastries, fruit, and coffee, and set the atmosphere with music. Your staff will look forward to this event each spring!

Catherine Trinkle, Hickory Elementary School, Avon, Indiana • March 2007

School-Specific Ready Reference

In order to make the library the ultimate place to go for information in the school, make a binder of all important school documents, and keep it at the circulation desk. Laminate copies of "ready reference" school papers such as the hall duty schedule, a master staff and student list, fire and lockdown drill procedures, faculty meeting schedules, team assignments, homeroom numbers and teachers, the school calendar, the code of conduct, and even the teachers' contracts. Staff members know that they can quickly pop into the library to find where a teacher is on hall duty, when our next faculty meeting is, or other important everyday bits of school information!

Jacquelyn Bertalon, Woodmere Middle School, Hewlett, New York • November/December 2008

Holiday Delights

After book orders arrive near the end of November, host a special staff day in the library called "Sweets and Treats Day." Decorate the library for the holidays. Invite staff members to have their lunch in the library on decorated tables. After their lunch, offer them a spread of homemade desserts. Display all of the new book purchases on surrounding tables and on tops of shelves. Let teachers preview and check out what's new for use in their classroom. As a parting gift, give staff members a small holiday gift from the library—usually a special bookmark, pin, or holiday antenna ball.

 Diane Howes, Pecan Valley Elementary School, San Antonio, Texas • November/December 2007

PROMOTING LIBRARY MATERIALS

Hear Ye!

Read aloud new or curriculum-related books at faculty meetings. This is an excellent way to model expressive reading and let your teachers know your high level of expertise in choosing appropriate books to use in the classroom.

 Catherine Trinkle, Hickory Elementary School,
Avon, Indiana • April/May 2007

Stalling New Materials

Create a word-processor document of newly arrived materials, with "Come check out our new materials!" in large bold letters across the bottom. Photocopy that page onto colored paper or paper with a pretty border so that it will stand out. Post these in the teacher restrooms on the back of the stall doors or on the paper towel dispensers. Our teachers soon come in asking for a book or video they've seen on the list, usually within the hour.

 Alicia Stratton, Jackson Road Elementary School,
Griffin, Georgia • April/May 2008

Celebrate New Resources with a New Arrivals Party

Have a "new arrivals" party at the beginning of the year to show off your new resources. Decorate a section of the media center with baby shower–related items such as balloons, streamers, posters, and inexpensive table center pieces. Invite students and staff by creating baby shower invitations and placing the invitations in all the teachers' mailboxes as well as posting them around the school. Refreshments are optional but will encourage more partygoers!

Melissa Allen, Glynn Academy Media Center,
Brunswick, Georgia • May/June 2009

Practice Makes Perfect

Make the faculty aware of all of the subscription databases at the beginning of the year. Then make it personal by periodically picking a different database that lends itself to a specific subject and introducing it to teachers in that subject area. Take screenshots and insert notes explaining some of the features. This works especially great for teachers of subjects such as art, foreign language, and so on who may not be aware of these resources.

Margaret Rowland, Cardinal Mooney High School,
Youngstown, Ohio • May/June 2009

Tick TOC

When you receive a new journal such as *Mailbox* or *Instructor*, make copies of the table of contents (if not prohibited by license) and put these in the teachers' mailboxes. Also put a copy in the principal's box. The teachers can easily scan the contents to see if there is anything they are interested in reading. I also put copies in a notebook with dividers for each periodical—no more thumbing through issue after back issue to find that article you were looking for!

Libby McGee, Tuloso-Midway Intermediate School,
Corpus Christi, Texas • November/December 2008

Promoting Your Professional Library

Organize new professional resources with labels—such as Poetry Resources for Language Arts, Math Assessment, Utilizing Technology in the Math Classroom, or even a specific content area that the material may address. Also display professional journals with sticky notes on the cover highlighting articles of interest. As an additional resource, you can include a folder for each teacher with helpful materials such as available audio/video resources in the media center, relevant content area Web sites, and even ideas or suggestions for collaboration.

 Stacy Symborski, D. R. Hill Middle School, Lyman, South Carolina • November/December 2008

WORKING TOGETHER

Let's Get Physical!

With two New Year's resolutions to keep this year—creating more opportunities for collaboration with my teachers and taking the time to exercise at least 30 minutes every day—I decided to try combining them! To ensure my commitment to these resolutions, I sent an e-mail announcing my resolution of walking the mile that surrounds our campus during the 35-minute lunch period each day and asked if anyone wanted to come along with me.

The first day, two teachers joined me for the walk, and I found that this uninterrupted time with them allowed me to get to know them better and to talk with them about their classroom activities (and how I could help them in the library). I now get e-mails from other teachers asking me to "wait" for them on specific days during the week when they want to join me on my walk. I'm not walking with the same teachers every day, but I am making a lot of appointments with different teachers who want to join me—and when I can meet alone with one or two teachers for 20 to 30 minutes each day with an opportunity to just talk about what's happening in their classrooms, the opportunities for collaboration are certain!

Shonda Brisco, Fort Worth (Texas) Country Day School
• August/September 2006

News for Teachers

Teachers at the elementary level typically send home a weekly newsletter, and you can too—for teachers. Devote one column to your weekly lessons and the standards they cover; other columns can cover book reviews, statistics, reading research, the Big6 or other research approach, a highlighted Web site of the week, and news on current education topics. Teachers will appreciate this form of communication.

Catherine Trinkle, Hickory Elementary School, Avon, Indiana • April/May 2007

Spread the Word

Bring professional books to your teachers. Check out professional books to "teacher's lounge," and keep them there for a couple of weeks. Then rotate them with other professional books you want your staff to be aware of. Busy teachers will appreciate the ease with which they can become familiar with this important part of the school's collection.

Catherine Trinkle, Hickory Elementary School, Avon, Indiana • August/September 2007

Banded Research Books

To help elementary students find information for reports while still allowing them to search the catalog and browse the shelves, plan with their teachers in advance. Then use seven-inch, neon-colored rubber bands to put on the front covers of all of the books that might be used as resources. Reshelve the books before the research begins. This indicates to your students in other classes that these books may not be checked out because they are being used for a special research project. Students have the materials they need and the authentic learning experience using the patron catalog that they need too.

Beverly Frett, Robert Clow Elementary School, Naperville, Illinois • November/December 2006

TEACHING TOGETHER

Collaborating through the Specials

No matter the type of schedule you have in your library (but especially if you are an elementary library media specialist tied to a rigid schedule that does not allow you to collaborate readily with classroom teachers), be sure to consider collaborations with the other "specialists" in your school. Many exciting collaborations can grow out of team-planning, team-teaching, and team-evaluating units of study in conjunction with your art, music, or physical education teachers—or all three of them together!

Toni Buzzeo, Buxton, Maine
• August/September 2006

Poetic Science

Collaboration is a great way to reinforce the science curriculum during a poetry unit in the library. At the end, students write astronomical poetry using the poetic forms and elements taught in the poetry unit, along with the facts and information learned in science. The kids really get into this challenging culminating activity.

Nelle Coleman Cox, Dover (Delaware) Air Base
Middle School • May/June 2009

USING TECHNOLOGY IN THE LIBRARY

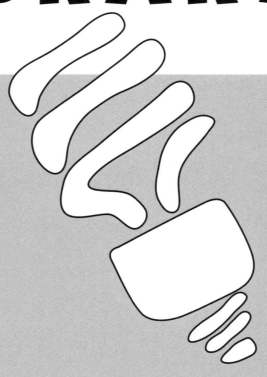

The use of technology has become so commonplace that the librarian could arguably boast "technology R us!" "Media specialist" is a term that encompasses the role the teacher-librarian plays. Media is embedded in the librarian's daily activities, from processing books and materials to checking out books to searching for reference resources. It adds a dynamic dimension to the skills she models for and teaches to students and staff. The librarian knows how to use online resources to bring learning to life. He uses electronic databases as well as search engines, wikis, blogs, and all things Web 2.0 to develop 21st-century learners. She must know how to problem-solve online when a student mistakenly finds a viral ad Web site and how to assist a teacher with using video software so that students can produce videos. She must know the difference between a USB cable and an S-video cord. Of course, this is in addition to tapping students' prior knowledge to teach 21st-century learning skills.

The tips in this section are divided into the following topics:

- Computers
- Printers and Printing
- E-mail
- Web Sites
- Searching the Internet
- Useful Library Applications

COMPUTERS

Smile, Your Error Message Is on Candid Camera!

Tired of writing down error messages to report computer problems to your tech team? Using 3 by 5-inch cards, write a number for each of the computers in your media center. When an issue crops up, hold the numbered card corresponding to the computer's number next to the screen and snap a digital picture of the error message. Attach it to your e-mail to tech support, or print and attach it to your school work order.

Judi Wollenziehn, Bishop Miege High School,
Shawnee Mission, Kansas • January/February 2009

iSight

If you have a Macintosh computer, click on the My Computer icon to see if you have Apple Built-in iSight. If you do, look at the top of your screen and press "Take a Picture." You will immediately see what students have been looking at all day. This can be a very sobering and humbling experience, but it also opens up a quick new world for taking student pictures with their favorite books to feature as wallpaper on your library browsers.

Sheryl Kindle Fullner, Nooksack Valley Middle School,
Everson, Washington • November/December 2008

Incredible Shrinking Text

To enlarge or decrease the size of text in a word processing document or Web site, hold down the control key and then use the wheel on the mouse to either enlarge text or make it smaller.

Anitra Gordon, Ann Arbor, Michigan • November/December 2007

PRINTERS AND PRINTING

A Printer by Any Other Name

We have had great success naming our printers from both a troubleshooting and a library fun standpoint. Each of our printers has a name label, so when there is a jam or need for paper refill, our students can come to us and quickly indicate which one is in trouble. I've known libraries that have named printers after famous libraries (Bodleian, Alexandria, or Library of Congress), but we have enjoyed shorter names (Lexi, Connie, Burt). It's a great idea for a contest ("Name the Library Printers!"), and students feel a great deal of ownership about the printer after it's named. When our students tell us about a paper jam, most of the time they'll say, "Lexi isn't feeling too well!"

 Courtney Lewis, Kirby Library, Wyoming Seminary Upper School, Kingston, Pennsylvania • November/December 2006

E-MAIL

PowerPoint PDF

To share a PowerPoint presentation on the Internet, save the presentation as a PDF document that can be viewed with Adobe Reader. The PDF presentation won't show such features as slide transitions or animations, but the information can easily be shared with anyone who has Internet access. PDFs can be viewed on Apple computers and older versions of Windows. If you use the "save as Web page" feature in Microsoft PowerPoint, only people with newer versions of Windows will be able to view the presentations.

Dawn Nakaoka, Kapalama Elementary School, Honolulu, Hawaii • August/September 2008

E-mail Binders

To prevent problems or heartache in the event that your e-mail server fails, print out messages you want to keep as soon as you read them. These may include confirmations of orders, important library or automation information, and so on. Three-hole punch the pages and arrange them in a binder, using dividers, in a manner that makes sense to you (e.g., date received, subject, or topic, etc.). You can periodically check through the binder and remove messages that are no longer needed.

Laura D'Amato, Parma (Ohio) City School District • August/September 2006

WEB SITES

Works Cited Solution

Confused about the proper way to document sources when doing research? Create a works cited page on your virtual library Web page. Include samples and instructions on how to document the resources your school provides as well as links to helpful Web sites. We followed MLA style but made some minor concessions to make the work easier for our students. Students now realize how important it is to give credit to the work of others and to follow a proper format. Because the guide is on the Web, it is always easy to use, even when students are working at home.

Carla L. Burmeister, Osseo-Fairchild Middle-High School Library, Osseo, Wisconsin • August/September 2007

Noting Great Web Sites

You probably belong to a variety of e-mail lists from which you receive e-mails filled with great ideas and suggested Web sites. Rather than stop your progress through a packed inbox to explore sites that seem interesting, keep a little notebook next to the computer. When a Web address appears tempting, jot it down in the notebook (or copy and paste it into a word processing document) and continue on with your e-mail. About once a week, set aside a little time to visit those sites and then decide which sites to bookmark or skip.

Lu Ann Staheli, Payson (Utah) Jr. High School
• January 2008

SEARCHING THE INTERNET

Web Scavenger Hunts on the Go!

Need a great way to get your students to visit educational and fact-filled Web sites at recess and break time? Have a stack of pre-made Web Scavenger Hunt cards available at the circulation desk. Color-code the cards according to subject using construction paper—for example, blue for language arts, pink for science, purple for social studies, and so on. Laminate the cards so that they will last longer. Now, when a student is caught visiting non-educational sites, you have a worthy e-alternative—and the student still gets to surf the net!

 Anna Saleme, Central Catholic High School, Morgan City, Louisiana • February 2007

USEFUL LIBRARY APPLICATIONS

Transferring Renaissance Records

Student records in any renaissance program can be easily exported and imported from any campus and to any campus. Simply select the student(s) by name under the school icon within the renaissance program you are using. At the top of the screen, select the student drop-down menu, select "export," and follow the prompts. Following the same steps, files can be imported. When students transfer from one school to another in district or across the country, their renaissance records can go with them electronically. Simply attach the file and e-mail it to the person responsible for renaissance programs on the new campus. Use your librarian skills to find contact information for the old school from which a student transferred to request records.

Kaylia Thomas, Marble Falls (Texas) Independent School District • April/May 2007

Freetranslation.com

If you occasionally have to type a foreign word with special punctuation such as Español with the tilde over the "n" or Frère with an accent grave, it can be exasperating to find the right program within word processing. Put http://freetranslation.com on your favorites list. Choose the language you want, and all the punctuation (attached to the letter) is at your fingertips. Copy the letter into your document, and it will match your font and size.

Sheryl Kindle Fullner, Nooksack Valley Middle School, Everson, Washington • August/September 2007

Fast Reading Level

There are many online sites that publish reading levels; however, I often run across a book not listed. I quickly type a paragraph into a Word document and hit spell check. At the end of spell check, the Flesch-Kincaid Reading level appears. This process takes less than a minute and can also be done by student or parent helpers.

Sheryl Kindle Fullner, Nooksack Valley Middle School, Everson, Washington • January 2006

ProQuest en Español

If you need resources in Spanish, try ProQuest. To pull up only articles written in Spanish, use the advanced search tab with "la(sp*)" as the first term and your subject as the second (or Boolean) term. Choosing Español from the dropdown menu in the top right corner of the ProQuest search page only changes the interface to Spanish. For example, "Search" would be changed to "Buscar," but the articles would still be in English unless "la(sp*)" is put into the search box.

Sheryl Kindle Fullner, Nooksack Valley Middle School, Everson, Washington • November/December 2006

PROMOTING READING

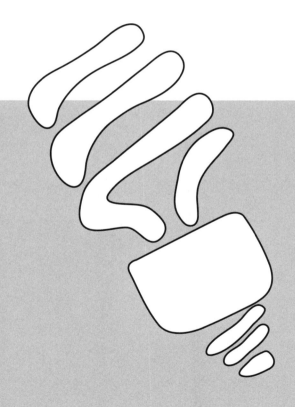

At the heart of her job is the librarian's love of reading. She displays this with every book talk, author's visit, Battle of the Books event, after-school book club, and bulletin board or book preview. Finding the right book and right tactic to encourage a reluctant reader or challenge a gifted student is a satisfying and rewarding experience that librarians relish. The confident librarian knows how to utilize displays, book previews on the library Web page, and student recommendations to convince all students that reading can be an exciting and revealing path to self-actualization. Hats off to promoting reading!

The tips in this section include the following:

- Story Times, Book Talks, and More
- Displays and Bulletin Boards
- Reading Incentives
- Student Recommendations
- Special Events
- Special Tactics
- Utilizing Technology

STORY TIMES, BOOK TALKS, AND MORE

Peas Try This!

When reading the book *The Monster Who Ate My Peas* (Peachtree, 2001), hide the cover and don't show the students the pictures until after you have read through the description of the monster. Tell them you want them to use their imaginations to visualize what the monster and other characters look like. Talk about chapter books not having pictures and about how important the author's descriptions are to give the reader an idea about the characters and setting. You can discuss how much fun it is when a movie comes out to see if you visualized things the way they appear in the movie. Finish reading the story without showing the pictures, and then have students draw what they imagine the monster looks like. After they finish, compare their drawings to the pictures in the book.

 Carol Crawford, Fort Lewis Elementary, Northside Middle School, Roanoke, Virginia • April/May 2007

Book Talks with Visual Aids

Sixth graders love book talks. To cover as many books as possible in one class period, set up four rectangular tables end-to-end in the front of the library media center. Create a backdrop for the books using a variety of shapes and sizes of empty boxes draped with colorful plastic sheeting. Place your new fiction books to be shared on bookstands at various elevations on the tables. Accompany each with an item representing the storyline. For example, Lasky's *Ga'Hoole* (Scholastic) series can have a stuffed toy owl and an owl call; *The Tale of Despereaux*

(Candlewick, 2003) can have a stuffed mouse with exaggerated felt ears. As you deliver your talk, have a helper parade in front of the watchful students with each book and item. The next day, get your reading teachers to ask the students, as a class, to recall as many of the items as possible in five minutes. Give prizes to the class with the best score. Multiple copies of your new titles will cover demand.

Connie Quirk, G. S. Mickelson Middle School,
Brookings, South Dakota • February 2006

Newbery Bingo

I had my students use 12 by 18-inch construction paper for the bingo boards. They cut up Follett Newbery posters into individual books and made Newbery bingo boards. The free space can be a book or the Newbery Medal from the poster. I didn't mind if each was different. I laminated them and use them for Newbery bingo each year. It's a great way to follow up with or even introduce Newbery Medal Books. I book-talk each book as I pick them. Save a poster to cut up for your bingo callout. I make new ones each year as new books win.

Lenore Piccoli, Mount Pleasant Elementary School, Livingston, New Jersey, November/December 2007

Pet Show

During a story time, *Pet Show* by Ezra Jack Keats is a great book to introduce your own pet show. Students make their own paper bag pet (real or imaginary) using scraps of paper, yarn, buttons, and glue. Make sure the paper bag flap is in the front for a mouth. Students write their pet's name and age and something special about their pet on the back. Make some awards with an Ellison letter machine (enough for each pet), and you're ready for your own pet show. Use a pretend microphone and have students come up for their interview, and the class can decide on the award prize together. Each pet gets claps and an award. Set up the video camera and watch afterward. It's a lot of fun!

 Lenore Piccoli, Mount Pleasant Elementary School,
Livingston, New Jersey • November/December 2007

DISPLAYS AND BULLETIN BOARDS

Guess Who?

At a faculty meeting, request time to read aloud *Knuffle Bunny: A Cautionary Tale* (Hyperion Books, 2004). Then ask staff members to bring a baby picture, a toy, or another item from their childhood and the name of their favorite childhood book. Display the pictures, items, and book titles in a secure location, and number each set. Challenge students to guess which collections belong to which staff members. Post the answers on an appointed date.

Aileen Kirkham, Decker Prairie Elementary School Library, Magnolia, Texas • April/May 2008

What's New This Week?

Have a theme of the week, such as dogs, water habitats, space, teeth, Australia, or hobbies. Create a simple book display each week highlighting books from your collection, perform book talks on the school-wide announcements, and list the titles each week in your school newsletter. Be sure to mention the Dewey numbers where students can find the books. This is an easy way to promote your collection and help students understand that the library is organized by putting books on a topic together on the shelves.

Catherine Trinkle, Hickory Elementary, Avon, Indiana • April/May 2008

Proper Display

A great way to get students' attention with a display is to have a "prop spot." Next to a book, put a prop that has to do with that book. Students' interest and curiosity will be piqued, and the book might just fly off the display the same day you put it up!

Tara LaCerra, Westmoor Elementary School, Northbrook, Illinois • February 2007

Brand New Books

If you are responsible for a large showcase (elementary or middle school), try a "New Edition" or "New Arrivals" display by posing your books in a doll's high chair, cradle, and carriage. If someone has a doll collection, you can also add dolls for interest.

Joan D. Villano, Fisher Middle School, Ewing, New Jersey • February 2007

Birthday Book Bulletin Board

Make a four-layer paper or felt cake in the style of the red and white hat displayed in *The Cat in the Hat.* Place on the wall with the title "Birthday Books." Each time a new book is "born into the library," add a candle to the cake with the name of the book and the date it was "born" so that students, parents, and staff can see what books are the latest and greatest to check out.

Aileen Kirkham, Decker Prairie Elementary School Library, Magnolia, Texas • February 2008

Everybody Reads!

A great way to motivate students to read is to have teachers and school staff members select a book they love from your collection. Use a digital camera to take a picture of them with the book of their choice in the library. Have staff members fill out a form giving a short statement of why they love the book they have selected. Add their quotes and graphics to the pictures using appropriate software to make 11 by 14-inch or 8½ by 11-inch colored posters. Once the posters are printed on a color copier, laminate them. Display the posters with the selected books. This is a great activity that classes can work on while in the library. Each class can be responsible for a different component of the activity, or classes can do all of the components but focus on different staff members (e.g., first grade teachers, science department, building service, etc.). Students could then check out those books, or the activity could end with a school-wide event. This is a great way for a library media specialist to collaborate with teachers, focus on information literacy skills, and get everybody at the school reading.

Laura Jeanette Brown, Montgomery County Public Schools, Center for Technology Innovation, Rockville, Maryland • March 2007

User-Friendly, Easily Updated Reading Lists

Students like to consult recommended reading lists to find reading material, especially when the lists connect them with books they've already read. Lists such as "If You Like *Go Ask Alice*" or lists that connect readers to books that are similar to favorite television shows are very popular. But making multiple photocopies of these lists can be time-consuming and wasteful, especially when the lists are updated regularly to include new additions. Instead, I make only one, full-color copy of each of list and place each page of the list in a plastic page protector that is linked with a metal ring. Because of the page protectors, the lists can be passed around without getting destroyed as easily, and I can update the pages regularly and easily. Binding them with metal rings allows me to hang them on pegs in the library for easy access.

Cathy Belben, Burlington-Edison High School, Burlington, Washington • October 2007

READING INCENTIVES

Library Happy Meals

Homes are awash with small toys from fast-food children's meals. Collect these for unusual incentives even for high school students. One current prize at our school is a joke—plastic that looks like a spilled latte or milkshake complete with a lid and straw. Solicit these from young parents or find them at garage sales for 10 cents each or less. For younger children, purchase white paper lunch bags and combine one toy with a barely used small book. Even kindergarten student helpers can stamp designs on the bags and fold or staple them shut.

Sheryl Kindle Fullner, Nooksack Valley Middle School, Everson, Washington • October 2008

Caught Ya!

To motivate students to read more, carry around a camera. When you catch someone reading, snap a picture of them. Put the photos on a bulletin board that says "Get caught reading." The students *love* it. After the picture comes down, I write on the back of it a little note encouraging them to read more and congratulating them on being "caught" reading!

Tara LaCerra, Westmoor Elementary School, Northbrook, Illinois • August/September 2006

Get Caught Reading!

Walk around the school and give small prizes for anyone who is actively reading a book. Prizes could be anything, including a bookmark, a pencil, or a piece of candy. Make sure students always have a book by placing a book display right at the entrance with face-front shelving. Keep the display full of new books and hot reads.

Melissa Allen, Glynn Academy,
Brunswick, Georgia • March 2008

Carried Away

Last year I had a reading program called "Get Carried Away with Books." During this time, each grade went to a different "destination," and they had to read a certain number of minutes to get there. There was a "mileage plus program" in which students could earn "miles" by writing postcards from where their hot air balloon was flying over (we had a map outside the LMC to track each grade with hot air balloons). When they reached their destination, we had a "themed" party. To kick it off, we had the teachers dress up and dance to a song from their destination, which was very exciting for the students! It was a huge success!

Tara LaCerra, Westmoor Elementary School,
Northbrook, Illinois • October 2006

Caught Reading

During the day in your library media center, keep an eye out for students engrossed in a book and take their picture. If you have an Ellison die cutout of a camera, place the student's picture in the center of the hole and write on the side of the cutout, "Look who was just caught reading!" Place these camera cutouts with pictures on the door of the LMC so all can see.

Diane P. Smithson, Old Donation Center,
Virginia Beach, Virginia • October 2007

STUDENT RECOMMENDATIONS

Book Recommendation Labels

Many of us welcome student suggestions for new books. When you receive the book a student suggested, place a book donation sticker in the front with the words, "This book was suggested for our library by _____" and include the student's name and the date. Students are pleased to see themselves recognized, and they take greater ownership in their library!

Tish Carpinelli, Lower Cape May Regional High School, Cape May, New Jersey • April/May 2007

Read Wallpaper

Take pictures of students with their favorite new books and post them as wallpaper on the library browsers. Horizontal pictures have less distortion. Limit photos to one or two persons so that titles show up well. I put a different picture on each browser and lengthen the amount of time before the screensaver kicks in. It's great for other kids to be greeted by those book-reading smiles.

Sheryl Fullner, Nooksack Valley Middle School, Everson, Washington • February 2008

Plate That Book

Whenever you order a book that was recommended by a student, teacher, or staff member, put a book plate designed by an art student inside the front cover, recognizing that person as the reason for purchasing the book. It could read "Suggested for your reading enjoyment by _____, Class of _____." Our students think it's great to have their names in the book.

Julie Burwinkel, Ursuline Academy,
Cincinnati, Ohio • January/February 2009

Book Display Reviews

Create a student book-review display. Take a picture of the student with the book being reviewed and place a speech balloon with his review next to the picture. Then place the book next to the photo and review.

Nelle Coleman Cox, Dover (Delaware)
Air Base Middle School • May/June 2009

Local Celebrities

Our local Kinko's donates a monthly 24 by 36-inch full-color "READ" poster (like the ones in ALA Graphics) featuring one of our students. I take the picture and format the poster file; Kinko's does the rest! Students select a few of their favorite books from our library media center for the display case, and I type a paragraph the student writes describing why reading is important in the student's life. This case is outside the door of the library media center, which is near the front entrance of the school, so it is highly visible.

Ellen Taylor, Rossview High School,
Clarksville, Tennessee • October 2006

SPECIAL EVENTS

Awards Celebration Party

As a culminating activity for a unit on the Newbery or Caldecott Award, have an Academy Award–style party to announce the winners! Students can make festive party hats, and a volunteer can make cupcakes to share. Decorate the library media center with streamers, balloons, and so on. The list of "nominees" can include the Honor Books and other student favorites as well as the medal-winning book. You can then announce, "And the winner is . . ." and state the name of the medal-winning book. Allow students to celebrate, but most importantly, have fun with this special day!

 Laura D'Amato, Library Media Specialist,
Parma, Ohio • August/September 2007

We ♥ Reading

Our February "We Love Reading" program encourages all students to track the number of pages they read during the month of February. We track the reading by grade level using heart cutouts for each 50 pages, color-coded by grade. We also encourage each student to donate one penny for each page he or she reads. At our school, this money is used to purchase new books for a local children's hospital. In our first year, we had 87 participants and raised $275 for new books! As students turn in their pledge forms, each receives an "I AM LOVED" pin donated by the Helzberg Foundation (http://www.iamloved.org). We put a bookplate in the donated books that says "Donated by the Students of XYZ Elementary. We Love Reading!"

 Danna DeMars, Garrett Elementary,
Hazelwood, Missouri • February 2008

Valentine's Day Readers Ready!

Work with classroom teachers to schedule read-alouds, with older students reading to classes of younger students as a Valentine's Day treat. Older students can read aloud a book and/or the Valentine cards to the younger ones. Announce grade levels who will be participating and thank them. Request that the following announcement be given on the read-aloud day.

> (Sing to the tune of "Mary Had a Little Lamb")
> *Valentine readers share good books, share good books, share good books.*
> *Valentine readers share good books; they'll share with you today.*

 Aileen Kirkham, Decker Prairie Elementary School Library, Magnolia, Texas • February 2008

Candy Reading Reminders

To celebrate National Library Week, Banned Book Week, Dr. Seuss's Birthday, or other significant events for your media center, give teachers a special treat and remind them just how wonderful it is to read. Type little notes on the computer and then cut these into small strips and attach them to a small piece of candy or other treat. Relate each note to reading and that specific kind of candy or treat. Following are some examples of sayings:

"Be a Smartie—read a book" attached to Smarties candies

"Don't be a dud—read a book" attached to a small individual box of Milk Duds

"Knowledge gained from books can be a real 'lifesaver'" attached to a small individual roll of Lifesavers

"Books can 'rock' your world!" attached to rock candy

"Reading is 'mint' to be fun" attached to a mint

"Don't be a sucker—read a book" attached to a lollipop

"Books are number 1, and pencils are number 2" attached to a pencil

"Just wanted to keep you 'posted' that this week is National Library Week [or other event]" attached to Post-it notes

Remember to let them know whom the treat is from with a short message such as "From the Media Center. Remember to celebrate National Library Week [or other event] by reading a good book."

Melissa Allen, Glynn Academy, Brunswick, Georgia, March/April 2009

Selling AR

If Accelerated Reader motivates a lot of your students at the book fair, put a sticky note on the shelves in front of each book that has an AR quiz, indicating the book level and number of points. Many students choose books that they can use for their AR goals.

Julie Ohrenberg, Pioneer Ridge Middle School, Independence, Missouri • March/April 2009

NLW Posters

In preparation for National Library Week, send out questionnaires via homerooms to all your middle school students. Ask the students to name their top three reasons to read and their favorite thing about the library. Their responses will be varied and often surprising. Make a list of the more creative answers and compile them into free verse poems (one or two poems per grade level depending on content ideas). Make posters of the finished poems and present them to the respective English teachers. Students are excited to see their own lines in print.

Connie Quirk, Mickelson Middle School, Brookings, South Dakota • March 2008

Happy Birthday, Dear Noah

Celebrate Noah Webster's birthday on October 16. Talk about the reason that dictionaries began (to standardize spelling) and then try reading the bit of *Frindle* by Andrew Clements (Aladdin, 1998) where Mrs. Granger loves the dictionary. Display types of dictionaries and talk about the career of a lexicographer. A fun activity is to remind the students that new words are added each year, and keep a bulletin board of suggestions for new words that could be added.

Lenore Piccoli, Mt. Pleasant Elementary School, Livingston, New Jersey • November/December 2009

SPECIAL TACTICS

Nonfiction for Primary Readers

My beginning readers love nonfiction books, but many of the nonfiction books have too many words on a page for these students to read. We pulled our easy nonfiction, looking for books with lots of white space, large fonts, and readable sentences, and put them on two separate shelves. Now when our kindergarten and first grade readers want nonfiction, they have their pick of readable books.

Karen Laabs, Viroqua (Wisconsin)
Elementary School • March 2008

Books for Underachievers

In middle school, I placed a sign by the picture books that read "Books to Read to Younger Brothers and Sisters." That way a student wasn't embarrassed to check out an easy picture book. He or she could always say it was for the young ones at home.

Linda Walkup, Tulsa (Oklahoma) Public Schools, Fulton Teaching and Learning Academy • August/September 2007

Book Series

For students who enjoy reading fiction books in a series, create a notebook arranged by author that you keep next to the card catalog computer at the front desk. Type the author's name at the top of the page and list books written by him or her. Then copy and paste the cover of each book from the Internet. This notebook makes a quick reference source when a student is reading a series and needs to know what book comes next. A good source for finding books in a series is http://www.fantasticfiction.com. After you print each page, use a three-hole punch and then place the page in the notebook.

Peggy Nance, Harrison (Arkansas)
High School Library • August/September 2007

Summer Book-Out

Send your library media center books on summer vacation. Students really appreciate access to your collection over the summer when they have more time to read. The Advanced Placement English students, for example, choose titles from the recommended list to prepare for the fall. Many take home the books they just couldn't find time to read during the school year. Simply set up a special due date two to three weeks into the next school year and check out the books. Advertise with a summer theme such as "Books for the Beach" or "Reading Fun in the Sun." Ask each student to sign a simple agreement and write down the number of books he or she takes home. Place a return box in the school office so that students can return the books over the summer. We started slowly by setting a limit of 10 books but now allow a maximum of 20 books per student. We have checked out more than 1,200 books over the past 12 years for summer reading, with very few problems.

Patricia Eloranta, Medford (Wisconsin) Area
Senior High School • January 2006

Series Reminders

Many books in a series are not labeled conveniently to help students know which books go next. Create custom bookmarks for popular series to assist avid readers. Each time a student says, "What come next in this series?" or "Which one is first?" hand out a bookmark to provide a quick and easy solution.

Janice Gumerman, Bingham Middle School,
Independence, Missouri • January 2008

Which Book Comes Next?

Our middle school students love to read series books. They were constantly asking which book came next until we came up with this solution. We typed lists of the books in each series, such as Harry Potter, Cirque du Freak, the Alice books, and so on, printed them on brightly colored paper, and either taped them directly to the shelves in front of a series of books or set them, in clear frames, right above a series of books. Now our students are easily able to keep track of which book they need next. I found a great list of series books at the Bettendorf Library Web page and was able to cut and paste with a minimum of time and effort. That Web address is http://www.bettendorflibrary.com/bpl-bin/series.pl.

Julie Ohrenberg, Pioneer Ridge Middle School, Independence, Missouri, January 2008

Active Read-Alouds

Instead of having older readers simply read to younger students, get them to connect to the text. Pass out picture books and have the older readers brainstorm questions for before, during, and after reading, to encourage active reading. Use sticky notes within the book. Keep a folder in the back of the book to house coloring pages and projects related to the text.

Nelle Coleman Cox, Dover (Delaware) Air Base
Middle School • January/February 2009

Author Letters, in Brief

Instead of having students write letters to busy authors, try a postcard activity. The skill of summarizing comes in handy when little space is available.

Nelle Coleman Cox, Dover (Delaware) Air Base
Middle School • March/April 2009

Looking for Read Alikes

To create a list of books that are "read alikes," use the 690 MARC tag (local subject). When you come across a book that strongly resembles a popular or classic title, create a "Read Also" 690 record for both the original and the read alike. As an example, for books that remind you of *Hatchet*, create a subject heading titled "Read also: Hatchet." Attach that as a site subject to each book that reminds you of *Hatchet* (including *Hatchet*). When you click on the "Read also: Hatchet" heading within the record, the entire list of books that "read alike" will appear. Do that for each book that has a "read alike" in your collection.

Elizabeth Mayer, H. B. Thompson Middle School,
Syosset, New York • March 2008

Remembering the Good Times

Don't you just hate it when students ask for a good book by genre and your mind goes blank? Keep a collection of hole-punched note cards listing the title, the author, and a brief annotation of the book on a ring by genre. It's easy to add cards to the file as we read new books. Use it often, and students will start using it before asking for help.

Debbie Clifford, Rachel Carson Middle School,
Herndon, Virginia • May/June 2009

Puzzle of the Day

Every morning, I write a puzzle of the day on the library whiteboard. I get most of the puzzle ideas from any number of brain puzzler books. The puzzles are usually a math or word problem. Students and staff both try to solve it each day. I have a basket of pencils, pens, erasers, mini posters, plastic rings, stickers, and so on to reward the winners who solve the puzzle. I always reward the first person of the day to solve it, and often, if it is a particularly hard one to solve, the first person each class period will get a prize. It's fun and inexpensive!

Kathleen A. Nester, Downingtown (Pennsylvania)
High School West Campus • October 2007

UTILIZING TECHNOLOGY

Kids Almanac PowerPoint

As a follow-up to teaching the *World Almanac for Kids* (World Almanac), create a PowerPoint of questions and answers (use a heading box and a text box for each slide). Students can review keywords by rereading the slide. Place the students in random teams; each student has an almanac, and anyone on the team may answer. Allow each team one strike (guess) before it is eliminated from the game. The team with the most points wins a prize for the day. You can have students create the questions/answers with page numbers from the almanac and use these for different classes.

Lenore Piccoli, Mount Pleasant Elementary School, Livingston, New Jersey • August/September 2007

Read Books, Save Lives

Students in grades 3 and up can improve their vocabulary while helping to end world hunger. Go to freerice.com to learn more about this computer game/program where sponsors donate 10 grains of rice to the United Nations to help feed hungry people. Scheduling a competition adds to the excitement, and the rice will just pile up.

Anitra Gordon, Ann Arbor, Michigan, January/February 2009

BUILDING POSITIVE PUBLIC RELATIONS

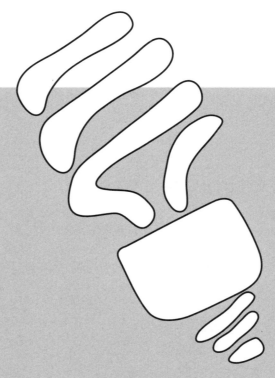

One of the most important roles of a librarian is that of public relations specialist and advocate for libraries. The librarian assumes this role and serves to carry the good news about libraries to the community, parents, students, and teachers on a regular basis. He promotes his media center and its programs because he dreams big and knows the support of these community members will go a long way in helping create libraries that meet the needs of all his patrons.

The tips in this section are divided into the following topics:

- Teachers and Staff
- Students
- Parents and Community
- Special Events
- Bulletin Boards and Displays

TEACHERS AND STAFF

Recycling for Faculty

Copier and printer paper with one side blank make great notebooks to use for taking notes at faculty meetings and workshops. Bind the paper using the spiral binding machines, and you can make any size you want, from full 8½ by 11-inch notepads to half-size or quarter-size notepads. You simply cut the spiral binder to match. You can use recycled card stock for covers. The binders can also be recycled when teachers are ready to throw away their "notebooks." This is a great task to give your student helpers. We also place quartered notepads at computer workstations. As an added touch, stamp the cover with your library information (name, address, phone number, and Web address).

Heather Loy, Wagener-Salley High School,
Wagener, South Carolina • August/September 2007

Pony Express

When a teacher e-mails a desperate plea for quick resources, deliver them. It is amazing the amount of goodwill that can be generated for your library by the simple act of putting materials on a teacher's desk instead of merely saying that they are available for pickup in the library or teacher's box. If necessary, commandeer a student as courier, but get the resources there with jaw-dropping promptness.

Sheryl Kindle Fullner, Nooksack Valley Middle School,
Everson, Washington • April/May 2008

Welcome Packets

To remind administrators and teachers of the importance of the library media program, create welcome packets introducing the library resources and services and latest library study information for new staff members. Including candy or other treats will make packets stand out!

Lindsay Weaver, Walnut Creek Elementary School,
Olentangy Local Schools, Columbus, Ohio • April/May 2007

Spoiling Teachers

Any teacher or volunteer who has a minor emergency heads for the library media center. We are fortunate to have an adult bathroom in our library media center. I keep it stocked with an SOS basket that contains hair spray, lotion, breath mints, a sewing kit, a simple first aid kit, safety pins, clear nail polish, hem tape, a lint brush, and deodorant spray. We keep feminine items under the table skirt. Chocolate, tea bags, and cocoa mix are kept in the office. The goodwill generated by our dollar-store purchases is well worth the expenditure.

Pat Miller, Sue Creech Elementary,
Katy ISD, Texas • January 2006

State of the Library Address

At the end of each month, create a State of the Library Address. With our principals looking to us for data on student learning, this is a great way to give relevant library data and information without overwhelming the administrator with facts and figures. This communication allows administrators to be well informed about library usage. It is also a great time to compliment teachers who have collaborated and used the library well, and it can include information about upcoming events and activities.

Lindsay Weaver, Walnut Creek Elementary School,
Columbus, Ohio • March 2007

Reaching Student Teachers

Looking for a way to connect with new student teachers? I invite them to the media center for a tour of the facility to show them how to search the OPAC and then highlight our district library media center Web site and spend a few minutes showing them how to use our online databases. I also explain some of the other services our media center offers. I provide printed copies of the media center Web site homepage and information with user names and passwords for home access to the databases. I ask the student teachers right off the bat if there's anything I can do to help them, and I check periodically throughout their time in the building to touch base with them. It's been a big success.

 Laura D'Amato, Thoreau Park Elementary, Renwood Elementary, Parma, Ohio • March 2006

Staff Photocopies for New Teachers

When making up goodie packages for new teachers each summer, always include a set of photocopies of your staff from the yearbook. With many teachers and administrators, new staff can sometimes be overwhelmed with names. This way, at least they can learn the teachers from their department, as well as have a reference for other staff. It is always a well-received welcome gift!

 Tish Carpinelli, Lower Cape May Regional High School, Cape May, New Jersey • March 2007

How about You?

Add a friendly reading nudge to your e-mail signature by including a line that reads, "I'm reading _____ _____ _____ by _____ _____. How about you?" It's fun to see what everyone is reading, and this serves as a model to everyone we communicate with, showing that we practice what we preach!

Brooks Spencer, Osceola Middle School,
Ocala, Florida • May/June 2009

LMC Welcome

For new teachers or student teachers, send a letter of welcome and an explanation of your LMC services. Also send a photocopy, taken from your most recent school yearbook, of your school staff—teachers, secretaries, custodians, everyone! This is a great way to meet each new addition to the staff because they invariably stop by the LMC to express thanks and to introduce themselves. I believe this icebreaker ensures they will return to us when the need arises.

Barbara Bomber, Northstar Middle School,
Eau Claire, Wisconsin • January 2007

STUDENTS

Student and/or Staff Recognition

Prior to students' taking state-mandated tests, post class lists in the workroom and request that staff members sign up next to individual student names to write each student a note of encouragement. Generate a list of adjectives so that you can make an original acrostic and add a note of encouragement.

Examples: Charlotte & Wilbur

Confident	**E**mpowered
Honorable	**W**onderful
Attentive	**I**ntelligent
Remarkable	**L**earned
Laudable	**B**rilliant
Outstanding	**U**nderstanding
Thoughtful	**R**espected
Tenacious	

Aileen Kirkham, Decker Prairie Elementary School Library, Magnolia, Texas, October 2008

Wall of Fame

Students love to look at themselves in pictures. In order to create an environment where students feel like they are a part of the library, clip student pictures from the local newspaper. Paste the pictures on colorful construction paper and create a "Wall of Fame." Students love to enter the library and locate their pictures on the wall. Keep the pictures on the wall for the current school year and then file the pictures by year. They come in handy for parent night and open house.

Jennifer Regel Parker, Magee (Mississippi) High School • August/September 2008

No One Goes Home Empty-Handed

My school was in a middle-class area with pockets of poverty. Our parent–teacher organization decided to help the children whose parents could not afford to purchase books at our annual book fair. Any child without book fair money was allowed to select one free book. At the end of the book fair, the cost of the "free" books for the needy students was subtracted from the profits.

Josephine Dervan, Retired, Strathmore Elementary School, Aberdeen, New Jersey • January/February 2009

Nickel Books

Place more books in student homes by accepting gently used book donations from the community. Create a Bargain Book Basket in the library where students can buy these books for a nickel. Children love to make purchases, and most students have five cents. They are so proud of books they can buy and keep. More books in student homes can increase opportunities for reading.

Marsha Holt, Southeast Fountain Elementary, Veedersburg, Indiana • January/February 2009

Summer Bookmarks

Before the end of the school year, make summer bookmarks for each grade level to showcase some of the favorite books for the year. Include the title and author of each book with additional sections for notable authors and some popular teen-read Web sites. Book-talk a few titles you know will get their attention. During the book talk, promote the public libraries and their summer reading programs.

 Leslie LaMastus, Frankford Middle School Librarian, Dallas, Texas • March 2008

Stuck on You

On 1 by 3-inch labels, print the URL of your library media center's electronic catalog. Attach these to the back side of bookmarks. Because the students love free bookmarks, chances are that someone along the way will see the URL at some time.

 Janice Gumerman, Bingham Middle School, Independence, Missouri • October 2006

PARENTS AND COMMUNITY

Donations at Book Fairs

During the book fair, my parent volunteers came up with the idea of labeling blank envelopes with the following information:

Reading Program Quiz Donations

Family Name _____

Child(ren)'s Name _____

Grade _____

Donation Amount _____

The money is kept separate from the book fair proceeds. With each book fair purchase, the cashiers ask if the family would like to make a computerized reading program donation. We've been able to order quite a few quizzes with this money. Writing thank-you notes to the families who donate is a good idea too.

 Aileen Kirkham, Decker Prairie Elementary School Library, Magnolia, Texas • March 2008

Summer Reading

For several years now, students, with their parents, have had the opportunity to take home a bag of books for summer reading. We have not lost a single book over the years. Each child can check out up to 15 books, but they cannot do this without parental permission and involvement. All of our students are bus riders, so we require that parents come to the library to sign the permission form and check out the books with their children. Parents take the books home in a special summer reading bag, along with a summer reading log and bookmark. A printout of borrowed books also goes into the bag. Parents agree to return the books during the first week of school. We provide information about summer office hours, so that if it became necessary, books can be returned to the office. Parents get involved in encouraging summer reading at the start of summer. They enjoy selecting books with their kids too. They've already started asking whether we'll be doing this again this year. And, of course, we will!

Beverly Golden, Canyon Ridge Elementary School,
San Antonio, Texas • April/May 2008

Outreach to Parents

How can librarians use parent conference days to their best advantage? Parents are very grateful to learn technology skills, at their own pace, with assistance available. Offer to teach parents to use the online databases. Include your invitation to the library with the letter sent to parents to schedule their appointments with teachers. Give parents a brief library orientation to the OPAC and to the location of books within the library. If school policy allows, issue them their own library card. Introduce them to the online databases, such as EBSCO or ProQuest, to show them how to find the latest issue of their favorite magazine. It is especially attractive to have the latest articles available online for free. Show them how to search for subjects, do a Boolean search, and use truncation. Give them time to explore the databases on their own and then offer to answer their questions. Pass out a printed sheet with all the passwords for them to take home. Have them sign in and write comments. Save these parents' comments in your portfolio for your evaluation. Alternatively, offer to attend a meeting of the parent association and present the lesson, as described here.

Barbara Herzog, Upper School Library, American School Foundation,
Mexico City, Mexico • January 2007

All-Generation Book Swap

Have a book swap that involves both students and parents. Put the books out on display and encourage parents and students to come to the library to participate in the book exchange. You will see young and old alike talking about their former books and inquiring about the new ones.

 Nelle Coleman Cox, Dover (Delaware) Air Base
Middle School • March/April 2009

Wishing for Amazon

Create an Amazon.com wish list for your school, and link the wish list to your library's home page so that virtual visitors can purchase librarian-selected items for the collection. Here's how:

- Create a new wish list at http://www.Amazon.com and then click on "Make this list public."

- Next, click on "Tell people about this list." The pop-up window asks, "How do you want to share your list?" You can choose to share via e-mail, by adding a button to your library's Web page, or by adding a widget showing recently added items to your Web page. This pop-up window also contains your wish list's unique URL.

- If you opt to add a button to your Web page, another pop-up window provides various icons and corresponding HTML code that may be copied and pasted into your Web page. Visitors to your site can now click on the button you've selected and visit your wish list.

Take advantage of the option to set the quantity desired, to set the priority for each item, and to add comments, such as "2008 Newbery Medal winner!" Don't forget to set your library's address as the mailing address for items purchased from this wish list (an option under "Edit list information"). And finally, promote your wish list at Back to School Night, PTA and Booster meetings, and even faculty meetings so that the entire community can support your library!

Amy V. Pickett, Ridley High School Librarian, Folsom, Pennsylvania, November/December 2008

Library Advisory Board Thank-You!

Free tote bags and giveaways that come from the exhibit hall at conferences are great for re-gifting. Put all the posters, sticky notes, bags, pens, and special doodads into a big box and let members of your

Library Advisory Board help themselves to the items. I had them pick a number out of a hat to determine their order so that it wasn't a free-for-all, and everyone was thrilled with coming away with freebies. It was a nice thank-you to a hardworking group!

Courtney Lewis, Wyoming Seminary Upper School,
Kingston, Pennsylvania • October 2006

SPECIAL EVENTS

Collect and Donate!

Because librarians should be ambassadors of goodwill and get along with everyone, why not extend this role to help others outside of school? Each month, I choose a charity and collect money from the staff that is donated to a worthy cause. After I send out a school-wide e-mail, I leave an envelope and staff roster in the office. In exchange for their donations, staff members may wear jeans on Friday. Our faculty suggests organizations that they would like to support. In the past, we have donated funds to the Lymphoma & Leukemia Society, Susan G. Komen for the Cure, the Multiple Sclerosis Society, the Alzheimer's Association, and many others. Everyone is happy to participate.

Gayle Stein, Central Avenue School,
Madison, New Jersey • October 2008

Photo Thank-You

I used to send thank-you cards after I had a guest reader in my library/media center. Now I take pictures of guests as they read to the kids and then use Microsoft Publisher to make a one-page poster as their "thank you." Just insert their picture above text that reads, "Thanks for helping us celebrate Book Week [or whatever the occasion might be] at [school name]" and the date. Present it to them so that they take their "thank you"—and a souvenir—with them.

Janella Knierim, Sugar Grove Elementary,
Terre Haute, Indiana • August/September 2008

Reading Slogans

To celebrate special events such as Teen Read Week or Children's Book Week in your library, have a contest for students to create reading slogans and illustrate them on bookmarks. Choose a winning design and make T-shirts featuring the slogan. Sell shirts to staff members and give T-shirts to students as prizes at an annual read-in. Decorate the media center with the most colorful bookmarks. Book club members can create giant-sized versions of some of the best bookmarks to really make the media center look festive. Kids love making the bookmarks and signs, and you can save the best ones to use year after year.

Marcia Kochel, Olson Middle School,
Bloomington, Minnesota • August/September 2007

Author Visit Memories

When an author visits, ask each student who has purchased a book for signing to let you take a picture of him or her with the author. If you take these pictures with a digital camera, it is easy to have prints made and well worth the nominal cost. Give the individual pictures to the students and encourage them to glue them into their signed books. This helps preserve a lasting memory of the special occasion and is good public relations for the library media center program.

Janice Gumerman, Bingham Middle School,
Independence, Missouri • February 2007

Can I Have Your Autograph?

For a recent author visit, I created a bookmark of an annotated list of the author's books appropriate for my students. Three bookmarks fit on a sheet of regular-sized paper. I then asked the author if she would sign the master and requested permission to copy these bookmarks on card stock to distribute to students. She agreed! I mailed the master to her home address, which she graciously supplied. After she returned the signed master, I photocopied this and passed out the signed bookmarks to the students who attended the author sessions. This way every student had a signed item, even if they did not purchase one of the author's books!

Janice Gumerman, Bingham Middle School,
Independence, Missouri • February 2008

Holiday Joy of Reading

Each year for Christmas, our local Chamber of Commerce gives food baskets to needy families in the community. The friends group of our library participates. The Friends receive the names and ages of all children in families receiving baskets. They use group funds to purchase an age-appropriate book for each child. The book and information about the library is included in the basket.

Josephine Dervan, Formerly at Strathmore School,
Aberdeen, New Jersey • November/December 2008

Bucks for Books!

Work with your principal, PTO, and/or community business partner to promote "Bucks for Books!" with a publicized need and specific goal. Generate a flyer with simple graphics. Show how many books the library currently owns and how many you need to be an exemplary library.

Aileen Kirkham, Decker Prairie Elementary School Library,
Magnolia, Texas • November/December 2008

BULLETIN BOARDS AND DISPLAYS

Teacher Feature Board

Because I review materials for *Library Media Connection,* I put a cover of the *LMC* magazine on the Teacher Feature board of the month. Each month members of the staff put up a poster sharing information about themselves and what they do, so I included the cover from the issue with my review and the page that had my review, as well as pictures of my family. I even included a brief information document in a folder for teachers or students who wanted to know more than just the pictures showed! The students and staff enjoy learning more about each other!

Sandy Scroggs, Schenck Elementary School,
San Antonio, Texas • August/September 2007

Display Case Trivia

Every month we create a new display case feature outside of the library. We tie our monthly homeroom trivia contest to the display case. For four days each month, we read a clue about a book over the announcements and ask students to bring their answer to the library. If a student is unsure of the correct answer, she can look in our display case for a clue. Sometimes, the book itself is mixed in with the other books on display, and sometimes we have an object that gives a hint as to the correct answer (for example, if the correct answer is *Tangerine* by

Edward Bloor, we might put a tangerine in the display case). The trivia contest has generated much interest in our display case.

Jackie Bertalon, Woodmere Middle School,
Hewlett, New York • November/December 2007

Teacher Feature

To get to know the teachers, create a "Teacher Feature." At the beginning of the year, ask the teachers and staff (including the principal) to sign up, and each week feature a different teacher with pictures from youth until present. Make sure to have their favorite book, "then" and "now," in the middle of the poster.

Tara LaCerra, Westmoor Elementary School,
Northbrook, Illinois • February 2007

WORKING
WITH
HELPERS

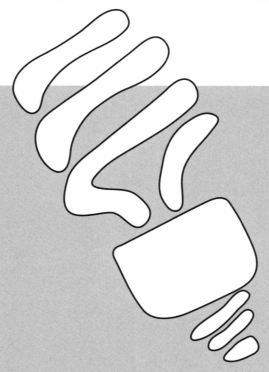

Student helpers and volunteers often provide the extra sets of hands a busy elementary librarian needs. These assistants and aides handle clerical work, run errands, and perform unexpected tasks that arise on a daily basis, leaving the librarian to teach and to make a difference for students and staff. These student volunteers and helpers can also add another element to an energy-filled, positive public relations program!

The tips in this section are divided into the following topics:

- Student Helpers
- Volunteers

STUDENT HELPERS

Recycle Those Badges

Save your badge holders from professional conferences to use for your student helpers. They are much sturdier than the plastic badges you purchase. We just hang our badges in an easily accessible place, and helpers know to grab one if they are running an errand.

Creedence Spreder, Salem High School,
Virginia Beach, Virginia • August/September 2008

Evaluating Student Library Aides

For library aides who will receive credit for their volunteerism, work with them using a point system. Give them a library skills assignment to complete, plus a journal to turn in each week. In the journal they record the tasks they have done each day, using good grammar and sentence structure and so on. Not only do they keep track of what they do, but they are also learning a job skill, given that many employers require employees to be accountable for their time. Assign points for each task, and determine grades by adding journal points to the assignment points.

Ruth Fies, Clark Middle/High School,
Hammond, Indiana • January/February 2009

Staff Badges

Library aide pins are costly, difficult to put on, and most of all *unhip*. We collected lanyards with ID pockets from various conferences and designed colorful inserts for our student workers—easy, cool, and free.

Sheryl Fullner, Nooksack Valley Middle School, Everson, Washington, March 2006

VOLUNTEERS

Volunteer Thank-You

Looking for an inexpensive and sweet way to thank your parent volunteers? Buy some chocolate candy bars. Then in PowerPoint draw a 5-inch by 6-inch rectangle. Add a text box for your kind words to express thanks. For example: "Wonderful Media Center Volunteer . . . We don't know what we'd do if you weren't here!" Add graphics, and change the font, color, and size as you like. Print and then cut out the rectangle. Place the rectangle over the chocolate bar and hold it together with tape. Present the gifts to your wonderful volunteers and show them your appreciation.

 Denise Dragash, Prairie Trace Elementary, Carmel, Indiana • August/September 2007

Gifts for Volunteers

To create a touching and inexpensive gift for your parent volunteers, ask the child of the parent volunteer for the name of his or her parent's favorite picture book—possibly one the child remembers reading with the parent at a younger age—and a sentence about what the student remembers most about the book. Find a picture of the cover of the book on the Internet and paste it into a word processing document, along with the quote from the parent volunteer's child, in a column format, leaving enough room to use a hole punch. Print the page using a color printer and then laminate it, hole-punch it at the top, and tie a cloth ribbon through the hole for a keepsake bookmark.

 Laura Stiles, Canyon Vista Middle School, Austin, Texas • February 2008

Love-Your-Volunteers Luncheon

Combine your volunteer celebration with a parent luncheon meeting held around Valentine's Day. Prior to the luncheon, order paperback books to give as gifts—each family represented gets one book. If you have a large Spanish population, order the same title in English and Spanish. You can cater the luncheon, or it can be potluck brought by the staff. Ask as many key staff as possible to greet and meet the parents.

Aileen Kirkham, Decker Prairie Elementary School Library, Magnolia, Texas • January 2008

Parent Volunteers Are a Treasure

Show your volunteers how much you "treasure" their help! Purchase a bag of Nestle Treasures chocolates. In Microsoft Publisher, use the business card template to create a cute tag reading, "We TREASURE our parent helpers at [name of your media center]." Copy the cards onto card stock. Attach the tags to the candy and place them in a plastic tub. As you greet or say good-bye to parent volunteers, hand them a piece of chocolate to sweeten the gesture and ensure they'll be back to help again soon!

Janette Fluharty, AIS East, Avon, Indiana • March/April 2009

Pamper Your Parent Helpers!

Make parent volunteers feel pampered and special when they come to help. Purchase a small plastic tote or basket and fill it with hand cream, Lifesavers, mints, chocolates, a bottle of water, and so on. Using Microsoft Publisher or Word, create an attractive thank-you sign and affix it to the side of the tote. Place the tote in a convenient spot and invite parents to help themselves to a little pampering as a sign of your appreciation!

Janette Fluharty, AIS East, Avon, Indiana • May/June 2009

ABOUT THE EDITOR

Kate Vande Brake is a newspaper journalist turned education public-relations specialist turned editorial consultant. Although her career path has resembled a pebble skipping across water, her love of reading and writing has sailed with her. Vande Brake's inspirations come from the simple pleasures of life—bright colors, slapstick humor, chocolate truffles—and she is often found teaching her three-year-old son the "important" things in life, like how to catch bugs and make jokes. She enjoys taking spontaneous trips to large warehouse stores with her husband where they can sample prepared convenience foods and try to leave without a pallet of unnecessary food. Vande Brake would be lost without her closest friends who call and e-mail her several times a week to make sure she is still smiling, and her heart belongs to her faith and her family who guide her through the obstacles of life and give her an overabundance of hope and joy to pass along to others. Vande Brake is also the editor of *TEAMS: Collaborative Units that Work*.

TIPS
OF YOUR OWN

_____

_____

_____

_____

_____

_____

_____

_____

_____

_____

_____

_____

_____

_____

_____

_____

_____

_____